BOY GENIUS

Boy Genius

Karl Rove, the Brains Behind the Remarkable Political Triumph of George W. Bush

Lou Dubose, Jan Reid, and Carl M. Cannon

PublicAffairs
New York

Composition by Mark McGarry, Texas Type & Book Works,
based on a design by Jennifer Dossin.

Library of Congress Control Number: 2002116766

ISBN 1-58648-192-4

FIRST EDITION
10 9 8 7 6 5 4 3 2 1

To Jeanne Goka, Michael, and Emiko
LD

To Dorothy Browne, Mark McKinnon,
and a genial patron saint of politics and writing,
the late Billie Lee Brammer
JR

To Raymond D. Strother, a Texan and a friend,
who opened my eyes to the rowdy ways
of political consultants
CMC

Contents

A Note on the Text

Lou Dubose, Jan Reid, and Carl M. Cannon acted as the co-authors for this book. Messrs. Dubose and Reid wrote Parts I and II and Mr. Cannon wrote Part III.

Prologue

Consider this tableau.

Fifteen flags posted along the back of a speakers platform provide the backdrop for a former secretary of state, a former chairman of the Republican Party, a former member of the National Security Council, the governor of Michigan, the senior U.S. senator from Georgia and four members of the U.S. House of Representatives. All their eyes are fixed on a figure as central to this scene as Christ was to Leonardo da Vinci's "Last Supper." The point of focus is George W. Bush, standing behind a lectern bearing the Seal of the Great State of Texas. He looks right and left, at the dignitaries flanking him. Then he turns his attention to the press pack that represents eighty-seven news outlets.

Seated among the reporters so he can watch the spectacle from their perspective is the strategist who directed both of Bush's campaigns for governor, as well as today's event: Karl Rove.

The figure at the center of Rove's set piece is neither a seasoned campaigner nor a practiced political tactician. Twenty years earlier George W. Bush lost a race for Congress in Amarillo, Texas. Five years earlier he was elected governor of a state where the governor cuts the ribbons while the lieutenant governor cuts the deals. And his foreign policy pronouncements about "Grecians," "Kosovarians" and "Timorians" are driving his poll ratings down even as they drive Jay Leno's Nielsen ratings up.

All this is momentarily forgotten by the reporters who sit transfixed before the Presentation of George W. Bush.

Bush is announcing only that he has formed an exploratory committee and will consider running for the presidency. Yet Robert Bryce of the *Texas Observer* writes of "an air of inevitability." *The New York Times* describes "a grand pageant of political might." To the reporters gathered in the Austin Convention Center ballroom, Bush already looks like a president, though the first primary is a year away. When Miriam Rozen of *The Dallas Observer* asks Rove why no reporter at the event has challenged Bush's limited understanding of national and foreign policy issues, Rove grins and responds: "Why didn't they do it? Because they were spellbound."

After the 2002 midterm election, the nation should be spellbound. Not only with President Bush, but with the man Texans have come to know as "Bush's brain" and whom the president himself calls "boy genius."

Karl Rove spent a quarter-century in Texas as a political consultant. But ask a politically aware Texan to name the one person who most altered the political landscape of the state over that same time period, and it's not likely that Karl Rove's name will come up. Pose the question in the form Rove himself might have, polling a random sample of potential voters, and it's even less likely that Rove's name will appear in the polling data. To most Texans—and now to most Americans—Karl Rove is a name they may have heard, without really knowing what he's done. But ask the same question of the 1,500 lobbyists who muscle their clients' bills through the Texas Legislature every two years, and Rove is at or near the top of every list. He also polls high with the capitol press corps in Austin, the bureaucrats who do the real work of government on legislative committees and regulatory agencies, and with elected officials.

Karl Rove is now in a category of major figures in American politics notable because the people in it are often relatively unknown. Rove is to George W. Bush what Kenny O'Donnell was to John F. Kennedy, what Michael Deaver was to Ronald Reagan, what Lee Atwater was to George H. W. Bush, and what James Carville was to Bill Clinton. As is true of most aspects of modern life, being behind the scenes these days is a lot more visible than it used to be. That's how James Carville got to be a national figure; now the same thing is happening to Karl Rove. The Boy Genius of Texas politics emerged from the tangle of the 2000 presidential contest to become an important figure in the White House. But it wasn't until George W. Bush's midterm election triumph that Rove became a celebrity of the first rank. Who is this fellow who guided the Republicans to the greatest midterm election victory of a president in modern times?

The role political consultants play in the shaping of American politics and public policy is enormous. Their ascendance could have been predicted forty years ago by a careful reading of Jane Jacobs' classic book, *The Death and Life of Great American Cities*. Jacobs lamented several technological changes that were transforming social life in America. Television and air conditioning were moving Americans away from their porches and public places and into their living rooms. Affordable cars and cheap gas were moving them out of the cities and into the suburbs.

Jacobs' book had nothing and everything to do with modern American politics. The changes she describes also created a new way of doing politics. Conversations about elections began to occur in living rooms, where they involve a television and a viewer. If political candidates could no longer talk to the voters of the suburban diaspora in labor unions and civic clubs, they could always catch them in front of their televisions. Or they could reach them through targeted mail drops, whose messages had been "polled and focus-grouped."

The immediate effects of those "conversations" are tested by overnight tracking polls, as close as you get to a real-time measure of how well a particular message resonates. Taken together, that all adds up to a sophisticated political conversation. Add a huge influx of money to the mix of television, direct mail, and polling, and the power of the professionals who master those media is evident. Political consultants are today's political bosses. They don't use the same means, but the ends are the same.

In the world of major league consultants today, Karl Rove has no peers. Just as no professional basketball player has ever performed at the level Michael Jordan reached when he was at the top of his game, no political consultant has ever played the high-stakes game of electoral politics like Rove does. Not Michael Deaver, not Lee Atwater, not James Carville. None of these "legends" was ever the dominant force in politics and policy that Karl Rove is today. His mastery of every aspect of modern politics—mail, television, polling, money, message, opposition research, electoral demographics—distinguishes him from others doing the same work. Other political professionals inevitably describe Rove through one of two martial metaphors. It's either war or chess. Rove either sets out to "conquer and destroy and takes no prisoners," or "sees the whole board and thinks twenty moves ahead." Like George Patton and Bobby Fischer, he has not been afraid to take risks with bold moves.

Karl Rove is the kind of political sage who knows how to make his candidate look good. George W. is a meet-and-greet master. But his grasp of the details of policy is often shaky. What Rove can do is figure out what Bush can say and to whom. Even more important, he understands how to move the pieces around on the chessboard so that the candidate on the attack is his and the one on the defensive is the other guy's, preferably a Democrat. George W. Bush has moved from a beginner in politics to the pinnacle based on a mix of things: luck, natural political skill, a conservative political tide, and shrewd strategic planning. The victory in Florida in the 2000 postelection added another component: outmaneuvering the opposition. But if Bush is the virtuoso, then Rove is the composer.

Looking back over Rove's career, a pattern emerges in which he focuses on the opponent and through a mix of the out-front and the underhanded, is able to win. Unlike Atwater who was mean and Carville who knew folksy, Rove is actually relatively low-key. He likes to remain behind the scenes, and underestimated. In the past, his opponents tended to overlook him until it was too late. But now, the candidate who Rove first helped in a losing campaign for a West Texas congressional seat is the Commander in Chief, and neither Rove's opponents nor the American public can afford to overlook him.

* * *

Rove got to where he is through a twenty-two-year political campaign of his own design. It was a campaign that began in Texas, and involved taking from the Democratic Party every statewide office and both houses of the Texas Legislature, and then redrawing the political map of the state to ensure that the Legislature remains in the control of the Republican Party.

When Rove first answered the call of George H. W. Bush to come to Houston and work for his political action committee, Texas was completely controlled by the Democratic Party. Every statewide office was held by a Democrat. Of the 181 seats in the Legislature, Republicans held only twenty-one. It had been over one hundred years since a Republican was elected governor.

But Rove saw the future, and it was "conservative white Democrats who are fed up with the liberal Democratic leadership at the state and national level, middle-class Hispanics who have become more independent and more conservative, and the migration to Texas of Republicans from other states."

Certainly, Texas was already changing when Rove got there in 1977. When Lyndon Johnson signed the Civil Rights Act in 1964 he said he feared that he had just delivered the South to the Republican Party. And so he had. But Rove anticipated that change before many Democrats in the state got wind of it. He became the agent of that change. He accelerated it. And he worked to ensure that the change was so profound that it is now almost structural.

Rove remade Texas in a way that observers of the 2002 midterm election victory will find familiar. He didn't wait for the right candidate for office to reveal himself; he recruited and created candidates. When the wrong candidate for a critical office revealed himself, Rove saw that the right candidate got the nomination.

Rove remade Texas in a way that observers of George W. Bush's defeat of John McCain in the South Carolina primary in 2000 will also find familiar, where it was alleged he used whispering campaigns conducted by surrogates to raise questions about an opponent's character.

In short, Rove remade Texas by methodically and ruthlessly eliminating the Democratic Party from the top down. He targeted Democratic candidates he believed he could defeat. He undermined them to make sure they would be defeated. He recruited Republican candidates who would win and remain in office. He lured conservative Democratic members of Congress into the Republican Party, with bankable promises of support in races for higher office.

And he delivered.

Rove learned his political skills in Texas, and Texas was a good place to practice. It's a state that comprises twenty media markets. If the state were an independent country—an idea that holds considerable appeal right now to Al Gore, John Kerry, John Edwards, and the other Democratic presidential contenders—it would be the eleventh largest economy in the world. Texas also defines the Wild West of campaign contributions. Any individual can contribute any amount to any candidate, as long as the contribution is declared with the proper agency in Austin. In 2002, the Democratic candidate for governor spent $64 million to lose the election—to a lieutenant governor who twelve years earlier had been recruited from the Democratic Party, repositioned, and run as a Republican—by Karl Rove. If there is a state in the nation in which to cultivate the fundamental political skill of raising and spending political cash, Texas is that state.

Now that Rove has moved from state politics to the national

stage, what might we expect of him? It is axiomatic to political journalists that the best method to predict what a politician will do is to look at the record. Rove's record is writ large on the state of Texas.

We need to understand where Rove came from, how he got so smart, what his relationship with Bush is about, what he stands for, what he wants, and what all this means to the people of the United States, because now it is us he is in charge of. Behind-the-scenes operatives are unique for their power in a democracy. None of us has any real voice in who they are or, unless they mess up, in getting rid of them.

This is Karl Rove's time.

PART 1

YOUNG REPUBLICAN

Gone to Texas

One morning in Austin in 2000, at a time when Karl Rove was just becoming a national political player, he stood in the airport holding a briefcase, awaiting a flight to Chicago. George W. Bush had a habit of assigning people nicknames, and he called the architect of his political career "Boy Genius" or "Turd Blossom," depending on his mood and the moment. It was a winter day, and the Republican master strategist—this was becoming his third moniker—was splendidly attired for the blast of cold that awaited him up north. Over his suit, white shirt, and tie he wore a beautiful cerulean wool overcoat that must have cost two thousand bucks and matched the blue of the Jaguar he drove. Rove was a stout figure, his blond hair combed straight back from a large gleaming forehead, and he wore tortoise-shell glasses. It was the hairstyle and affect of none other than John Dean, that snitch and betrayer of Rove's first and lifelong hero, Richard Nixon. Within the surplus pounds Rove possessed the same kind of baby-faced handsomeness. He was at ease among his fellow travelers but was also remote from them. He reeked of power, and carried himself like a man who knew he was making history.

Traveling with Rove was Mark McKinnon, one of his many admirers. Though nominally still a Democrat, McKinnon had fallen under the spell of Bush and had signed on, as long as the team would have him, as producer of the Republican candidate's TV ads. Once a liberal hellion and country-western songwriter on the staff of Kris Kristofferson, McKinnon had worked as a young press aide and speechwriter for a Democratic governor of Texas named Mark White. Rove's first big success in Texas politics had been at the helm of the gubernatorial campaign of Bill Clements, the roughneck Republican who trounced White in 1986 after having surrendered the office to him four years before. "Karl wiped the floor with us," McKinnon joked of that misbegotten race. Four years later, McKinnon was the campaign co-manager in the first leg of Ann Richards' winning campaign for governor. George W. Bush's surprising demolition of Richards in 1994, of course, vaulted Rove to national prominence and positioned his candidate to seek the White House. McKinnon had seen first-hand what Rove brought to a political campaign—from the losing side. Now he wanted to be on Rove's team.

McKinnon observed Rove's pose of hauteur with a smile, as he asked a friend and colleague from the Richards days (at the airport to catch a different flight) if he would like to meet the famous consultant. The man's body language answered for him: not particularly. Bush might be a decent and charming fellow, but Rove had a nasty reputation among the liberal Texas Democrats he had for years put to rout.

McKinnon countered that working with Rove the politico was like watching Bobby Fischer play chess. Rove saw the whole board and was always several moves ahead. "He is a master of everything," McKinnon said, exploring other metaphors. "Most great political minds can understand strategy, media, and polling, but not all the little parts—budget, scheduling, mail, fundraising. It's the difference between driving the car and being able to take apart the engine when something goes wrong." McKinnon surmised: "When the President was growing up, he wanted to be Willie Mays. But when Karl was growing up, he wanted to be senior adviser to the President."

Once, during a panel discussion hosted by a conservative think tank, the American Enterprise Institute, the moderator asked Rove when his obsession with being on the inside of presidential power and history began. Rove's comeback was unhesitating: "December 25, 1950." It was the day he was born.

Karl Christian Rove was a Christmas child, born in Denver. When the doctor whacked him, he probably yelped "I Like Ike!" Rove was Republican as soon as he could formulate the thought, though Dwight Eisenhower may have been a little soft around the edges for him. As a little boy Karl was always thinking, always reading, ever the eager student. That could be a burden in Sparks, Nevada, and other towns out West where he grew up. Rove was hardly born to country clubs. A grandfather had labored on a highway crew during the Depression; his mother once lived in a tar paper shack with walls patched with newspaper and flour paste. His dad was a geologist prospecting for zinc, lead, uranium, copper, and molybdenum, so they moved around a lot. Then, as now, the West was largely Republican. Rove was born into the cold war, to the menace of world communism, and he seemed to comprehend at once the importance of knowing one's enemies and how their minds work.

As a grade-schooler he wrote a paper on dialectical materialism. "A complete nerd," he described himself, many years later, when it was not so painful. With burr haircut and glasses, he would put on a white shirt and tie and hurry off to grade school carrying his first briefcase. He had a brother named Eric, and a sister, Reba. Reba said the three of them used to play a game called "See if You Can Stump Karl." His brother would read a passage from a book Karl had consumed the week before. The trick was for Karl to guess which word his older brother left out. One of the first books he read was titled *Great Moments in History*. For a long time, he always kept his worn and cherished copy of the book with him.

"My parents were totally apolitical," Rove said. "I have no idea why I was not." In 1960, in Arvada, Colorado, young Karl announced that Richard Nixon ought to be president. Eisenhower's vice president was a Californian, and he was intense in a way the old general was not. He thrust his chin out and shook his finger in impromptu debate with the Soviet leader Nikita Khrushchev. Khrushchev was a frightening man whose anti-American belligerence had driven him to pound a podium at the United Nations and threaten the West by stating that "We will bury you." Rove spoke up for Nixon to a girl who lived across the street and who preferred John F. Kennedy. She let go a roundhouse and decked Karl. She was older and bigger, which perhaps soothed his wounded pride.

At age eleven, according to his dad, he was visiting an aunt in Minnesota and dashed through a police barricade at a parade so he could get an autograph of a governor. He dreamed of being president, and was elected class president in junior high and high school. He had a big poster above his bed that said, "Wake Up America." The Western states were spawning a militant far-right conservatism, and groups like the John Birch Society perceived in socialist ideology a danger to the country that was traitorous and omnipresent. Kennedy's glamour was lost on teenagers like Karl.

After Nixon lost the 1960 presidential race and went on to lose the governor's race in California two years later, he was replaced as the unblemished star of the right by a jut-jawed U.S. senator from Arizona named Barry Goldwater. Goldwater had written a book called *The Conscience of a Conservative* that would become an American political classic. "Extremism in the defense of liberty is no vice," he proclaimed. Goldwater cast aside the Republican establishment, then personified by the progressive New York govenor Nelson Rockefeller, and rode a crest of emotion to the party's presidential nomination in 1964. His campaign slogan was "In your heart you know he's right." Goldwater was a hero to young conservatives; his ideological purity was an inspiration. But the world had tottered on the brink of nuclear war during the Cuban Missile Crisis, and then Kennedy had been assassinated in Dallas, a hotbed of the far right. By 1964 right-wing extremism had lost some of its allure. The Democratic nominee, President Lyndon Johnson, successfully cast Goldwater as a loose cannon who might lead the nation to a nuclear apocalypse; by contrast, Johnson appeared reasonable and restrained, a steady leader in a troubled time. When the sun set in the mountain time zone, the 1964 presidential election was already over; Johnson had buried Goldwater's far-right campaign.

Rove went to Olympus High School in Holladay, Utah. One friend recalled him fondly as "the biggest dweeb" in school. A teacher and LBJ Democrat named Evan Tolman recognized Rove's intelligence and talent and told him that to get an A in social studies he would have to volunteer for the campaign of his choice. He became a youth coordinator in the 1968 reelection campaign of Republican Senator Wallace F. Bennett. He worked as a volunteer at the campaign office and mobilized crowds of like-minded teens at rallies.

Across the country, protesters were taking to the streets, screaming obscenities about the Vietnam War; urban ghettos were erupting in anarchy and flames; the guns of assassins were ringing out. In the midst of this turmoil, Republicanism was a rock of steadiness. Richard Nixon might not have had the charisma of Barry Goldwater, but he proved to be a much better politician. This time Nixon got it right and he was elected president, which made the fall of 1968 doubly sweet for Rove: Senator Bennett won as well.

In a state dominated by Mormons, Rove grew up in a household without religion. His best friend and debating partner later said that this seemed to bother Rove, but for whatever reason, religion never took with him—despite its importance to his politics and many of his candidates.

Rove's father traveled a lot for his work, and the marriage of his parents was rocky. Just as the A-student and class president was about to leave home and make his way in the world, his dad walked out for the last time on Christmas, Karl's birthday. His mom got a divorce in Reno. Years later, when the children were grown, she committed suicide.

Rove was like a character in a Charles Dickens novel. At much too young an age he had to start living by his wits and designing his own future. In the spring of 1969 he was admitted to an honors program at the University of Utah in Salt Lake City. He had a $1,000-a-year scholarship from the William Randolph Hearst Foundation. That wasn't enough to live on, of course. He waited tables in a dorm and got a gun stuck in his face one night while working in a convenience store.

For a while, he later said with amusement, he manned a cash register in a shop thick with that perfume of hippies, patchouli oil. The period's wild ride of sex, drugs, and rock 'n' roll wasn't for him. He escaped the Vietnam draft, but loathed everything those anti-war protesters on TV stood for. If this was an ideological inconsistency, he never dwelled on it; and it was one he would share with hawks like Dick Cheney and Paul Wolfowitz. "I came from a relatively conservative state, Utah, and it was hard to sympathize with all those Commies," Rove explained.

Rove loved American presidential history. He devoured tales about Andrew Jackson and Theodore Roosevelt. His college mentor, a political scientist named J. D. Williams, said of Rove: "He could write well. He had good organizational skills, and he had a very clear love of victory. Politics was his varsity sport."

Rove might have gone on to the academic career that seemed to beckon, except that electoral politics was a lot more fun. By 1970, Rove had dropped out of college and moved to Illinois. The decision to leave school was a measure of his rise in young Republican politics, signaling no loss of intellectual ambition. Everett Dirksen, Illinois' colorful, gravel-voiced U.S. senator, had just died, and Rove was hired to organize young Republicans for Dirksen's appointed successor, the soon-to-be-forgotten Ralph Tyler Smith. Bob Kjellander, then president of the College Republicans at the University of Illinois and prominent in the national party, described the Westerner's arrival for *The Boston Globe*: "He was incredibly energetic and full of ideas. He was a ball of fire. He could get kids motivated, and you have to remember that was the height of the Vietnam War.

Being a Republican on a college campus in 1970 was not popular, but Karl motivated people and got them working."

Rove also picked up some "down-ballot" work—that is, work for candidates for lesser offices, which are listed below the presidential and gubernatorial races on a ballot. A Democrat named Alan J. Dixon, who would later make it to the U.S. Senate, was running for Illinois state treasurer that year. Pretending to volunteer for the campaign, Rove got into Dixon's office and swiped some letterhead. He wrote a letter and mailed 1,000 copies, even distributing it among skid-row bums, inviting them to Dixon's campaign headquarters for "free beer, free food, girls and a good time for nothing." It was just a dumb prank, he insisted when his authorship of the letter was exposed. It was a youthful indiscretion, he said, but the episode would hound him.

Rove headed for Washington in the summer of 1971 and got a plum job, considering that just two years earlier he had been a broke student working a cash register. He was hired as the paid executive director of the College Republicans, which was run by the national Republican party. The following year, Nixon destroyed George McGovern in the presidential race, using dirty tricks to do so even when they weren't necessary, and then embarked on a strategy of paying his enemies back. The loyal Republican Rove absorbed one of Nixon's guiding convictions: The end always justified the means. In Washington Rove ran with a GOP firebrand from South Carolina, Lee Atwater, who would later rise to fame as a renowned strategist—and attack dog—for Ronald Reagan and the elder George Bush. They talked politics, endlessly, but then Atwater would be at the center of a social hubbub, listening to blues music on the radio and collecting phone numbers from young women, as the shyer Rove held back. "I guess I'm more cerebral and lack his great people skills," Rove would say of his friend. "And I'm more of a nerd. Lee was a nerd in high school, but then he learned to play the guitar and talk to girls, and I never did. That's serious."

Rove was always self-deprecating, in that way. But David Tyson, another of the young Republicans then in Washington and later a crucial Rove ally in West Virginia, remembered their crowd: "This was a group of people who were conservative, sharp, and aggressive, but Karl stood out. He was more mature, more poised, than the rest of us." Tyson elaborated: "Even at that stage of the game, he had command of what was going on. Some of the College Republicans were just there to socialize, but Rove was there to work."

Rove was twenty-two now. The lack of a college degree on his résumé nagged at him, and he took courses at George Mason University, in a Virginia suburb of the capital. Still, he was on a fast-track in GOP politics. In 1973 he ran for national chairman of the College Republicans. His opponent was Terry Dolan, who would later found the National Conservative Political Action Committee, the direct-mail and soft-money machine that helped vault Ronald Reagan to the presidency. Rove always said the contest for head of the College Republicans was one of belief and direction, not just intra-party ambition. Rove was heir to the pragmatic Nixon, who would break with traditional Republicans to seduce the Teamsters and establish diplomatic ties with Red China. Dolan was the rigid ideologue who wanted to ban abortion and coddle the Christian right. The choice for voters on college campuses was a stark one.

In the contest for the chairmanship, Dolan's allies included Charlie Black, Paul Manafort, and Roger Stone, all of whom rose to power as whiz kids, policy advisers, and fundraisers for Reagan. But Rove had Atwater as his chief strategist and manager of the South. They raced around the country in Rove's brown Pinto; Atwater turning on the charm with the girls. In the end it was no contest. Rove beat Dolan, 63 votes to 5.

But an ugly thing called Watergate was loose in the land, poisoning the atmosphere—especially in Washington. George H. W. Bush had been a Houston congressman, a failed U.S. Senate candidate, and an ambassador to the United Nations. Now he took on the thankless task of directing the Republican National Committee as the accusations worsened, John Dean sang, and the Nixon presidency came apart. A then-little-noted sidebar of *The Washington Post*'s Watergate coverage maintained that a young politico named Karl Rove had conducted training sessions for College Republicans on the nuance and technique of Nixon-style dirty tricks. A scandal involving collegiate Republicans was all George Bush needed. Nixon by then had been forced to resign the presidency—an extremely bitter pill for Rove to swallow—in part because of similar allegations. The *Post*'s story carried enough weight that Bush felt compelled to send an FBI agent to question the young man. Rove was horrified by the public stain on his reputation. He owned up to the childish prank he'd pulled in Illinois, but swore that the alleged training sessions were a foul lie planted by his rival Terry Dolan. Out West, Rove's sister Reba remembered her brother making long and frequent phone calls to their mother, assuring her of his innocence: "He just kept telling her and Dad that he didn't do it." After a month of internal inquiry, the national party cleared Rove and ratified him as the collegiate chairman, but Reba believed that the incident permanently spoiled her brother's appetite for being the candidate himself.

In 1974 Rove got his first job as a real campaign manager, directing a congressional race in Nebraska. But he was quickly back in Washington, where Bush put him to work. Watching Nixon go down had been painful for Bush, whose Republican ties ran deep. The GOP needed to be rebuilt, and if Rove's résumé suggested anything, it was loyalty and a willingness to work for the party, no matter how tarnished its image. Rove took a job as special assistant to Bush.

After Gerald Ford was defeated by Jimmy Carter in the 1976 presidential election, Bush cast his eyes on the White House, knowing that Ronald Reagan, the former governor of California, would be his strongest rival. In Houston, Bush's master strategist, the sleek attorney James A. Baker III, had formed The Fund for Limited Government. It was a political action committee—a new type of organization proposed by Congress as an antidote to the abuses of Watergate. But for Republicans as well as Democrats, PACs had quickly become fronts for raising vast campaign war chests, and Bush and the Texans didn't mean to be outspent by Reagan and his Californians. Impressed by Rove's work for the party, Bush picked him to go to Houston and direct his PAC.

Rove left Washington and the verdant Virginia countryside for the Southwest in 1977, his future bright before him. For an avid student of American history, the move was rich in precedent: Sam Houston, Davy Crockett—all the intrepid souls who had gone out west to find their fortunes, in rattling wagons painted with the letters "GTT." *Gone to Texas.*

2

The Future in Plain Sight

When he was still working at Republican party headquarters, Rove was sometimes called upon to run errands for the party bosses. Though his political talent was obvious, he was still young, and such dues-paying was a part of the routine for even the most ambitious. So there was nothing particularly unusual about Rove being asked to deliver a set of car keys to the son of a party functionary. The dashing young bachelor who would be driving the purple AMC Gremlin with denim-blue seats was visiting from Harvard, where he was getting his MBA.

Years later, Rove would still vividly remember the first time he handed a set of keys to George W. Bush: "Huge amounts of charisma, swagger, cowboy boots, flight jacket, wonderful smile, just charisma—you know, wow."

In 1978, as Rove was joining James Baker III and the senior Bush's political action committee in Houston, George W. was in the West Texas town of Midland. His father had made his first million dollars in the oil field there, and Bush returned hoping to do the same. He had been working as a landman, a class of oilpatch dealmakers who pore over deed records in search of mineral rights to purchase for oil and gas leases. In fact had gone as far as incorporating his own small oil exploration company, when a veteran Democratic congressman announced his retirement. Bush, who had recently married a Midland school librarian named Laura Welch, decided to run for the open seat. He told friends who were surprised about his sudden interest in politics that he feared that under President Jimmy Carter the "United States was heading for a European-style socialism."

Bush entered the Republican primary runoff to face Jim Reese, who had been the mayor of Odessa, the blue-collar twin city that provided drilling company executives in Midland a steady supply of roughnecks and roustabouts. Reese had since become a stockbroker. He attacked Bush for his father's association with the CIA and the Trilateral Commission, an organization of government and business leaders from the United States, Europe, and Japan, whose existence stirred the suspicions of many conservatives. He also went after Rove, mailing out a letter warning that Bush had "Rockefeller Republicans such as Karl Rove" working on his campaign. Bush denied it, telling the *Midland Reporter-Telegram* that Rove was "a young twenty-seven-year-old guy who works in my Dad's office in Houston. He has nothing to do with my campaign. I doubt if he even supports Rockefeller." It would be many years before Bush would admit that Rove was in fact involved in his campaign—albeit in a limited way.

Bush won the primary to face Democratic state Senator Kent Hance in the general election. Hance made an issue of Bush's huge fundraising advantage ($400,000 to $175,000), claiming that much of the money came from outside the congressional district. He painted Bush as a child of privilege who had attended prep school in Andover, Massachusetts, and had graduated from Yale and Harvard. His stump speech included an elaborate story in which he described the driver of a car very similar to Bush's asking a local resident for directions to a nearby ranch. He is told to go about a mile, turn left, and then look for the cattle guard. Wanting to make sure he won't miss it, the driver asks one further question: "Now, what color uniform is this cattle guard wearing?" In addition to being funny, the story painted a vivid picture of Bush as a clueless, carpet-bagging Yankee.

For his part, Bush misread his constituents and supported the grain embargo that blocked the sale of Texas High Plains wheat to the Soviet Union. Sure, the locals were against communism, but bidness was bidness. Then, on the eve of the election, Bush was blindsided by a mailing sent out by a Hance supporter criticizing a "Bush Bash" at Texas Tech University in Hance's hometown of Lubbock. "Dear Fellow Christians" the letter began. It went on to detail an ad in the Texas Tech newspaper that promised "free beer" at a Bush political rally. Hance won 53 percent of the vote.

It was a textbook example of how to lose an election. Bush's campaign was hastily put together and made poor use of the money advantage it enjoyed. Bush allowed his opponent to define him, and he did a poor job of defining himself. Ads of the candidate jogging suggested that Bush was out of touch with the Texas Panhandle in 1978, where pedestrians of any sort were viewed with suspicion, if not alarm. Rove, whose involvement in the campaign was limited to a volunteer role as an adviser, but who watched the race intently, must have winced when Hance "went negative" on Bush late in the campaign, inadvertently echoing the fake "free beer" flyer Rove had used to tarnish Alan J. Dixon eight years earlier. But no Rove campaign would ever again make the blunders made in Bush's 1978 congressional campaign. In fact, with the exception of running against a much-better-funded opponent, Hance's winning campaign looked much like the campaigns Rove would run in the future.

Bush learned his lessons from the campaign as well. After losing, he told his opponent, "Hance, you had a message and you stayed with it." That the "message" had less to do with policy than it did with personal attacks might not have escaped Bush's attention.

Not long after his loss to Hance, George W. Bush was unwinding at a backyard dinner party in an Austin neighborhood north of the University of Texas campus—geographically speaking, the very heart of Texas Democratic liberalism. Bush and his wife, Laura, had come as guests of one of her oldest friends from Midland, who now made her home there.

Bush was no doubt pleased and proud of the obvious stir his attractive young wife caused in the group, which included reporters, professors, and trial lawyers. Most of these people were Democrats, but Bush was relaxed, friendly, and nonchalant about his defeat by Kent Hance in the West Texas race for Congress.

"What's your dad doing now?" one man asked politely.

"Running for president," came the genial reply.

The man blinked. Slight smiles and eye rolls were exchanged among the other guests.

George Bush? President of the United States?

Texas Democrats might not have felt the ground shifting beneath their feet, but Karl Rove was convinced he did. Working in Houston for Bush and Baker's PAC, Rove was emerging in Texas GOP circles as a wizard of the political technique known as direct mail. He crafted letters with underlined zingers that fired up partisans to get involved, sign up, and write fat checks. Just as important, he had an instinctive and highly-developed gift for knowing to whom to send those letters. At the same time, Rove was building the foundation for a political consulting firm that he hoped would enrich him as well as bring him power. Tom Cole, a major player in the national GOP party structure, later said: "He had the idea that someday Texas would be a Republican state, and he wanted to be there at the beginning. That was a brilliant political insight, but it was an even more brilliant business insight. He got himself ready for something he saw was coming. He planned from the start to be the dominant guy in the emerging Republican Party in the second biggest state in the country. That's the political equivalent of deciding to be Microsoft."

Texas certainly seemed to be moving his way. Though the younger Bush had lost his impulsive run for Congress, that same fall saw the diminutive U.S. Senator John Tower, a state Republican pioneer, win a tough reelection race.

Liberals had been apathetic about the Democratic nominee, a professorial congressman named Bob Krueger, and turnout was low. But Tower was pulled across the finish line by a new partisan fervor, rallied by an effective phone-bank operation that had also fired the governor's race. The Republican candidate for governor, Dallas oilman Bill Clements, had launched his campaign by flinging a toy chicken across a banquet table at his startled opponent, the overconfident attorney general John Hill, and declaring that he, Clements, was going to tie Jimmy Carter around Hill's neck like a dead rooster tied to a dog. Clements delivered on his boast.

Bill Clements had built his oil company around friendships with men who had been his teammates on a state champion high school football team in Highland Park, the lily-white enclave of old-Dallas wealth and privilege. That season had been played a long time ago, when football helmets were still made of leather, but even after all those years, the old-timers' loyalties and estimates of each others' abilities never wavered. Clements would use his own wealth and the support of his friends to underwrite his campaign, and it was a formidable combination.

Clements was everything the genteel Yankee George H. W. Bush was not. Unapologetically unrefined, he was a Texcentric worthy of a cameo in a Larry McMurtry novel: rich, rough-hewn, outrageous, outspoken. He drove a blue Mercury station wagon with imitation wood paneling, and his sartorial signature was a windowpane-plaid sports jacket. And he was a Republican in a predominantly Democratic state. Any political consultant could have bent your ear for an hour explaining why there was no way to elect Bill Clements governor.

And yet Karl Rove did it. Twice.

Clements was Rove's first client as an independent political consultant, and it was Clements' first campaign that anticipated the rise of the Christian right. In 1978, Texas was a Democratic state, and a dull Democratic attorney general named John Hill was the odds-on favorite to win the governor's race. But Hill had shut down a Christian boys' home in South Texas, after discovering that the boys living there had been subjected to beatings with pine paddles, enforced kneeling for hours on hardwood floors, and solitary confinement while listening to hours of their pastor's recorded sermons. Though he was only doing his job, Hill's civil suit cost him the election.

Lester Roloff, the Baptist preacher who ran the home, began urging evangelicals to vote for "Brother Bill" Clements, making appeals on his radio program and barnstorming the state in the small Cessna he would later pilot into the hereafter. Christian crossover voters provided the 18,000-vote margin that defeated the Democratic attorney general. After his election, Clements took Brother Roloff's side in the lawsuit, describing Hill's legal action against the Christian boys' home as "nitpicking."

Rove was in transition from working for Bush in Houston and running his own campaigns in Austin. He worked on Clements' campaign but was not nearly as central to it as he would be to his subsequent runs for governor. But Rove saw the future in Bill Clements' 1978 win.

Clements was the first Republican governor since Reconstruction, elected in a state that had been a Democratic Party franchise for more than a century. At the time, Republicans held one of the state's two U.S. Senate seats, two of its eighteen U.S. House seats, and eighteen of 150 Texas House seats. Only three of the thirty-one state senators were Republicans, and none of the twenty-two statewide offices was occupied by a Republican. Until Bill Clements defeated John Hill.

After several Texas Republican Party funders saw what Clements had pulled off in 1978, they decided to begin raising money for his second election campaign. Like Clements, Bum Bright had played high school football at Highland Park. And like Clements, he had gone to work as an oilfield roughneck and later built a company, or several companies, that made him a millionaire. Bright was putting his money into two Texas institutions: Texas A&M University and the Republican Party. In 1979, he called Rove and offered him a job raising money for Bill Clements.

Rove would later recall that at the time, Texas Republicans didn't recognize the potential for raising money in the state: "I still have the piece of paper that Bum Bright gave me on the budget. They wanted $200,000 in two years from direct mail because they had 5,000 donors in the '78 campaign. And they were very dubious about direct mail."

By the end of the first year Rove had expanded the donor list to 44,000 names and raised $1 million for Clements. The state was a huge pool of conservative money that hadn't been explored or exploited.

American electoral politics were changing, and old-style political operatives like George Parr, the South Texas political patrón who helped Lyndon Johnson steal an election from Coke Stevenson two years before Karl Rove was born, had all but disappeared. Voters were moving away from the political organizations that had once been influential in the cities and were most easily reached by two types of media: direct mail and television. Computerized databases made targeted direct mail a powerful political tool, and Rove—always an autodidact—was quickly teaching himself how to use direct mail, mail that raised money and got a candidate's message into homes.

Rove even walked a business journal through the process: "Write the plan, position the client, write the copy, secure the list, design the package, supervise and (or) generate some of the production here and then we set up a system to analyze response to understand what worked and what didn't." It was a pared-down description of the complex process that has become such a science that direct-mail consultants can predict within a fraction of a percentage what the return on a particular mailing will be.

It was not quantum physics. But Rove achieved a success with it that had not been previously seen in Texas. "Karl was the right guy at the right time," said Bill Miller, an Austin political consultant who has worked with and against Rove. "He was here in the late seventies, with Bill Clements. He was the guy who began collecting the names of the people who gave the money."

In 1980, Rove accepted a job as Clements' chief of staff and threw himself into the complicated work of legislative redistricting, sometimes working in alliance with conservative Democrats. But most of what the Republicans gained would be lost in a court challenge of the new districts. Another disappointment came in his personal life. That same year, his marriage of four years to Valerie Wainwright, the daughter of a prominent Houston family, ended. And when Clements asked Rove for a five-year commitment, the young politico balked, telling Clements he wanted to start his own business. Karl Rove + Company opened its doors in Austin with one client: Bill Clements. In raising money for Clements, Rove saw a more important function than working in the administration of a governor restrained by a Democratic House and Senate and nine Democratic justices on the nine-member state Supreme Court.

Rove had several backers in his business venture. The most important, because of his deep pockets and commitment to the Republican Party, was a polo-playing millionaire rancher named Tobin Armstrong, whose wife Anne had been the national Republican party co-chair when Rove worked at the Republican National Committee. Anne Armstrong had been elected Republican National Committeewoman from Texas in 1968, when the party was still a small elite group of intruders in a territory controlled by Democrats. By 1971 she was co-chair of the RNC and had worked in the Nixon White House. Tobin Armstrong's backing gave Rove's fledgling business the imprimatur of the state's monied Republican aristocracy.

With Rove handling his direct mail, Clements was in even better political shape for his 1982 reelection bid against Mark White, the tall, drawling, centrist attorney general who had replaced John Hill. White was hardly an electrifying campaigner, and Rove and his fellow strategists had every reason to believe they would have four more years of a governor around whom they were building a Republican Party that could at last compete with the Democrats for statewide offices. But Clements' election had shocked Texas Democrats and gotten their attention. Lyndon Johnson, after all, was not too long dead. The establishment Democrats who learned the ropes and wielded power during the LBJ years might move easily in country clubs with Bush, Baker, or Clements, but they weren't just going to roll over and hand the prize to a bunch of Young Republicans. The patrician U.S. Senator Lloyd Bentsen was up for reelection in 1982, and so was the popular Democratic lieutenant governor, Bill Hobby, a Houston newspaper owner and son of a distinguished Texas governor. Cut from another mold but spoiling for the brawl was Jim Mattox, a pugnacious, labor-backed Dallas congressman running for attorney general.

Another force for the Democrats was Bob Bullock, the rambunctious comptroller. He came out of a milieu of roadside beer taverns, jukebox suppliers, and streetfighters in small towns south and east of Dallas, roots he shared with the aspiring country singer and sometime Bible salesman Willie Nelson. Bullock graduated from the Texas legislature to lobbying for car dealers to an appointment as secretary of state—a patronage post doled out as a reward for political service to the governor, in this case Preston Smith. Bullock told a story about Archer Parr, heir to the political machine that delivered the legendary mystery box of votes to LBJ in 1948, saying Parr offered Bullock a $5,000 donation to Governor Smith in the form of a check from the local school district. A careful bagman, Bullock insisted on cash, whereupon Parr walked into a bank, cashed the check, and handed Bullock the stack of bills.

Bullock ran for comptroller and won in 1974. The comptroller ran the tax-collecting agency, an obscure office that few Texans seemed to be aware existed. Bullock set out to make it the agency that drove fiscal policy in Texas, and by the end of his first year in office there was no doubting its existence. He personally led raids on businesses that were delinquent on their taxes, after conscientiously alerting the press. The pictures of state employees carting away the ill-gotten gains of tax scofflaws made for entertaining journalism, and Bullock made headlines crowing about how much money he was recovering for the taxpayers of Texas. Bullock modernized the agency, hauling in computers and buying planes, which he used to fly to other states for the ostensible purpose of seeing how other tax agencies worked. He opened offices in towns far from the capital, which served the legitimate purpose of pursuing the agency's business across the state and which also served as the infrastructure of his nascent political machine. Bullock understood that knowledge is power, and in the manner of Lyndon Johnson he had the goods on everybody, keeping a meticulous system of card files on both allies and enemies.

Bullock hired the best and the brightest and paid them better than anyone else in state government, and they earned every penny. He was notorious for what one state senator referred to as "drive-by ass-chewings." These often climaxed with the on-the-spot firing of the offending employee, who would inevitably be awakened the next morning by a phone call from Bullock demanding to know why the hell he wasn't at work. Bullock chain-smoked and worked hard and drank hard, and his inner circle of favorites were expected to keep his hours, which involved long days and longer nights.

One night early on in his career, Bullock wandered out of an Austin bar and, thinking to catch a quick nap before driving home, climbed in the back seat of what proved to be the wrong car. He woke up in bewilderment to find himself being driven through the dark city streets by a total stranger. Rallying, he thrust a hand over the seat and introduced himself to the driver, scaring the poor man out of his wits: "Hi there!" he boomed. "I'm your secretary of state!"

Another backseat tale, perhaps apocryphal, had a Manhattan cabbie zooming through stoplights and traffic, deaf to Bullock's sozzled protests from the back seat. Exasperated, the comptroller was said to have finally produced a pistol and stuck it in the cabbie's ear, roaring "I told you to slow down!"

A larger-than-life figure, Bullock cajoled and bullied people in equal measure, depending on his mood and what he needed from them, and his generosity and meanness were equally outsized. In Texas, Bullock was legendary. And he was feared.

These were the veterans aligned against Clements and the GOP recruits that fall of 1982. In their confidence and resolve to prove the state had turned Republican, party strategists ditched the strategy of picking just a few races and concentrating on them. They put up candidates for races up and down the statewide ballot, and even recruited opponents to San Antonio's veteran Democratic congressman Henry Gonzales and Houston's charismatic two-term congressman Mickey Leland, who were shoo-ins for reelection. Hardly cowed, ambitious Democrats battled each other for chances to get in the fight. One was Garry Mauro, who had upset a West Texas state senator in the Democratic primary and was running for land commissioner at the age of thirty-two. Curly-haired, handsome, and full of himself, Mauro had carried the bags and driven the car in the last campaign of the old liberal warhorse and LBJ nemesis

Ralph Yarborough, and in 1972 Mauro had befriended Bill Clinton and Hillary Rodham when Gary Hart sent them over from Arkansas to run George McGovern's doomed presidential campaign in Texas. Another Democrat was Jim Hightower, the Stetson-wearing candidate for agriculture commissioner. Bone-thin and a fount of one-liners, Hightower could be a skillful demagogue, when that was useful. He too had worked for Yarborough, and in the leftward presidential campaign of Oklahoma U.S. Senator Fred Harris; as editor of the liberal muckraking *Texas Observer*, he had railed against establishment banking, industry, and agriculture. The Democrats' candidate for treasurer, Ann Richards, was then married to a prominent civil rights and labor lawyer; she had been among the luncheon crowd of Dallas supporters John F. Kennedy was riding toward when he was assassinated in 1963. After her family moved to Austin, Richards emerged as the chief aide to state representative Sarah Weddington, the attorney who successfully argued *Roe v. Wade* before the U.S. Supreme Court. Richards had first won office as a county commissioner in Austin. Liberals and the local press loved her.

Texas was booming in 1982. The price of oil shot toward $30 a barrel, and the state sat on vast reserves of natural gas. A popular bumper sticker crowed: "Freeze a Yankee in the Dark." With the overflow energy money, instant real estate tycoons were flipping land, putting up high-rises. They thought boom times would never end. Instead of getting symbolic credit for the good times, the oil-patch millionaire Clements began to look like a stodgy figure stuck in the past. Impressed by data-bank work that had helped Fort Worth congressman Jim Wright survive a close race, an Austin political consultant named Jack Martin put the computer wizards to work for the Democratic slate. For once the Democrats ran as a team: They coordinated their schedules and in a rare show of discipline said only nice things about each other. The money and the heft that Lloyd Bentsen and Bill Hobby brought to the Democrats exposed the weakness of the Republican candidates who were down-ballot from Clements.

That October Karl Rove experienced the tremors underfoot and the sudden desperate free-fall that he would later engineer so often for enemies and rivals.

If Mickey Leland and Henry Gonzales had been unopposed, their supporters might have stayed home. Instead they voted, and they didn't split tickets for the Republicans. Turnout reached 50 percent—extremely high in Texas—and when it was over the GOP takeover of the state lay in shambles. Running behind a flood of money unleashed by the pro-business Senator Bentsen, White beat Clements going away. Bullock and the other old-guard candidates brushed their opponents aside; it was a Democratic sweep from top to bottom. In a parade on inauguration night the following January, a photographer caught Garry Mauro, with a mane of hair like an Italian playboy; Jim Hightower, with his boots, mustache, and sly country boy grin; and Ann Richards in high heels, looking like she was dancing a country two-step, hand flung in the air. Three aspiring stars of a kind never before seen in Texas, each of them aware of the rivalry of the others.

For a Republican drawn into party activism by the presidential candidacy and conservative philosophy of Barry Goldwater, the Democrats' heralded Class of '82 must have been horrifying.

It took Rove a while, but one by one, he picked them off.

3

Whatever Happened to the Class of '82?

Texas Democrats would never again see anything similar to the sweep of 1982—the state party's last great year. Rove was fiercely loyal to Bill Clements, whom he considered a real trailblazer and who had put his personal wealth into a race he was not supposed to win. Though Rove worked hard to reelect Clements, the 1982 loss was not entirely unexpected. Rove understood the power of money, incumbency, and organization in an election, and he knew that Bentsen was a formidable force in Texas politics. He was a wealthy Anglo patrón from the Lower Rio Grande Valley who had served in the U.S. House and had defeated liberal U.S. Senator Ralph Yarborough in the 1970 Democratic primary—a campaign as aggressive in tactics and in issues as anything Rove had yet put together. Flush with campaign cash, Bentsen carried the Democrats' 1982 ticket into office with him.

But the tide of electoral politics in Texas favored Rove. In 1983, Democrat Phil Gramm switched parties and was bold enough to resign his U.S. House seat and run again as a Republican. Gramm got a little help from his political consultant, Karl Rove, who ushered him into the Republican Party and then organized his successful reelection campaign against liberal humorist John Henry Faulk. Gramm became the only member of Congress in the twentieth century to resign and then successfully seek reelection as a member of another party. The Reagan landslide of 1984 helped Rove elect Gramm to the U.S. Senate seat opened up by John Tower's decision not to run for a fifth term. Rove ran a bruising, negative campaign against liberal Austin state senator Lloyd Doggett, whom Gramm easily defeated. Rove also managed to get another Karl Rove + Company client into office: Dallas-area Congressman Joe Barton. Joining Gramm and Barton in the state's Republican congressional delegation was West Texas Congressman Kent Hance, who as a Democrat had defeated George W. Bush in a race for congress six years earlier. "Karl was instrumental in my changing parties," Hance said. "He said, 'Look, the Democrats are never going to help you, you're too conservative. You'll find a warm welcome in the Republican Party.' I don't think he was acting as an emissary of the party; he was just giving me his opinion."

By 1985 the Rove + Company client list that once included only Bill Clements had grown to eighteen. And the staff in the office northwest of the Capitol complex had grown from three to ten. The Texas Republican Party was a growth industry.

Rove admired Clements because he had been first. "His personal resources made it possible for him to promise victory-starved Republicans that he wouldn't run out of gas like Republican candidates had done in the closing months of other campaigns," Rove said in a speech quoted in the *Austin American-Statesman.* Yet when Clements talked about running again in 1986, Rove wasn't among his early supporters. The Dallas oilman was sixty-eight. He had a bad hip—"a hitch in his get-along," he called it—which aggravated his congenital bad temper. He was not an easily managed candidate, nor so attractive that he was an easy sell to voters. Rove saw the future of the party in younger politicians like Gramm and Hance, who Rove believed should be the party's next candidate for governor. Hance was closer in age to Governor Mark White, eager to run for statewide office, and Rove had told him he would run his campaign. But when Clements announced his intention to run, Rove found himself conflicted. "He's a loyal person," recalled Hance. "I was going to run for governor and he had agreed to help me. He had been with Clements and he came to me and said 'I've gotta go back to Clements; Clements gave me my start.'"

Chinks were starting to show in White's armor. He had enlisted H. Ross Perot to put together an ambitious education reform program, which was now in effect across the state. To improve the quality of instruction, all teachers were now required to pass competency tests. To improve student performance in the state's secondary schools, all students participating in extracurricular activities were subject to a "no pass, no play" rule, under which students who were failing classes were barred from participating in nonacademic school activities. In a state where football is the focus of small-town social life and an annual rite of passage for young men, valuable players who didn't make the grade were suddenly spending their Friday nights in the stands with the losers from the National Honor Society. High school coaches in the state's 1,000-plus independent school districts pasted red stick-on dots to their wristwatches as reminders to vote against White, and complained to their booster clubs that Governor Mark White and H. Ross Perot were destroying Texas football.

The incumbent governor faced more than angry coaches. The price of oil had plummeted at a time when the state was still heavily dependent on the oil and gas severance tax. The recession had settled in far beyond the oilpatch. Unemployment was hovering at 10 percent, the highest in the nation. It was no time to run as an incumbent. So Rove's client, the old oilman setting out to recapture the office he'd lost four years earlier, began the race with a double-digit advantage.

But White summoned the legislature to Austin for a special session and passed a temporary sales-tax increase that would allow the state to meet its obligations and would expire when the economy recovered. If it wasn't Solomonic, it was as good as governing gets in a state where the governor has extremely limited powers and the absence of an income tax imposes drastic limits on government services. White's poll numbers turned upward so quickly that one Austin political consultant compared the comeback to Lazarus' return from the dead.

A month out, the race was a dead heat and anyone not focused on the Division 4A state football championship was wondering if the one big debate between the two candidates would decide the governor's race. The younger Democratic governor was expected to dominate the cranky old oilman. Clements had served a term as governor, but White was the candidate who better understood policy and politics. Clements' experience was in the Texas oilfields. Political handicappers predicted he would be embarrassed in a debate with White. Even if he survived, the trend in the polls favored the incumbent—as did the public perception that White had resolved the fiscal crisis in Austin.

But a funny thing happened on the way to the forum in Houston, where the two candidates were scheduled to meet. On the morning before the debate, Karl Rove held a press conference and announced that an electronic eavesdropping device had been discovered in his office. Clements' deputy campaign director, John

Weaver, described the incident as "Texasgate" and lamented that politics in the state had become so degraded that these "irregularities" could become commonplace.

Suddenly, an acrimonious debate about clandestine bugging displaced the news coverage of the debate. Stories about the incident overshadowed campaign issues like education, taxes, and crime, and shifted the media's attention away from White's comeback in the polls. Rove accused no one. But he told reporters that the only one with anything to gain from knowing what was said in his office was Mark White or the political operatives running his campaign. "Obviously, I don't know who did this," Rove said. "But there is no doubt in my mind that the only ones who would benefit from this detailed, sensitive information would be the political opposition."

There was something odd about the crime. Usually, when someone discovers their office has been broken into, they call the police. Rove called a press conference.

Rove and his campaign staff began to tell the story that they had hired a private security firm to sweep their office after *Dallas Morning News* reporter Sam Attlesey asked a question that included information so specific it could only have come from inside the campaign. Rove was certain that one fact the reporter referred to had been uttered only once, while Rove talked on his office telephone four feet from the framed red-white-and-blue needlepoint Republican elephant behind which the bug was discovered.

When the FBI finally got involved, the *Morning News* reporter told agents that the source of information about the Clements campaign was Washington Democratic consultant Harris Diamond. A political reporter at the competing *Dallas Times-Herald* got the same information from the same source. The openness with which

Diamond was talking to the press did not suggest he was a conduit for information obtained by a hidden listening device. Diamond said no one had to go to the extreme of bugging an office to find the information he'd been feeding to reporters, which had to do with the Clements campaign's television advertising budget. Most of it was readily available in a weekly media report released in New York.

The other piece of highly sensitive information that supposedly got loose via illicit electronic means was that Lee Atwater—Rove's friend and political mentor—was being asked to come to Texas. Atwater had earned a reputation for vicious attack ads aimed at "driving up the negatives" of his opponents, and for devious campaign tactics. Rove wondered how anyone outside his office could know about Atwater's plans.

As it turned out, Atwater would never make it to Texas. But Rove's plan to bring him in, according to another Clements aide, was a "closely guarded campaign secret." Rove had been talking to the Alexandria, Virginia, consulting firm of Black, Manafort, Stone & Atwater. But, Rove alleged, no one outside his office could have known that. Diamond laughed at the notion that such information could be kept under wraps in the tightly-knit world of political consultants in the nation's capital. "It's all over Washington," Diamond said. Everyone in the business knew that Clements was not satisfied with the work of his national media consultant and had approached the firm Atwater worked for.

To the White campaign media director, the bugging looked like a setup. "I am absolutely confident that our campaign had absolutely nothing to do with this," said Mark McKinnon. "I think by thinking this would be a news story, they thought strategically that they would have something to gain from this." McKinnon complained that the "whole thing stinks and the wind is blowing from the Clements campaign." Rove had blown his early twenty-point lead in the polls and the race was even, McKinnon said. Someone in the Clements campaign operation had resorted to a stunt to provide cover for their collapsing campaign.

And then the story broke the day before the debate.

No one ever proved who planted the listening device. But it was not, as Rove had implied, the White campaign. "We were first on the scene and concluded that Rove had hired a company to debug his office and the same company had planted the bug," said a source in the Travis County District Attorney's office. The *Dallas Morning News* used the Freedom of Information Act to obtain FBI memos that also pointed to Rove's private investigators. The FBI had concluded the firm hired to sweep the office planted the listening device there.

Yet no charges were filed and, after the private investigator Rove hired received a "target letter" advising him a federal grand jury was considering charges against him, the investigation ended. Democrats complained that the investigation disappeared into the Reagan Justice Department. They argued that Rove's relationship with Vice President George Bush made it unlikely that the Justice Department would take any further action.

Did the news coverage of the bugging and the public perception that the White campaign was responsible turn the election in the direction of Rove's client? "It got a lot of play in the newspapers the month before the election," said White campaign director Dwayne Hollman. Hollman said he would have preferred to see the focus kept on the candidates and the issues at a critical moment in the campaign when White was pulling ahead.

Close to the end of the race, the Clements campaign mailed out
what appeared to be a newspaper to voters in certain parts of the
state. It included an account of Mark White's arrest for driving
while intoxicated—years earlier, when he was a college student. Jim
Hightower, the Democratic Agriculture Commissioner, tried to find
some humor in it. "Clements is guilty of DWI today," Hightower
said. "Driving while ignorant." Maybe the laughter eased the pain
for White. He came into the election knowing it would be a fight.
He never expected that someone would dig up an ancient DWI. Nor
did he think someone would imply he had bugged his opponent's
office.

The story about the bugging stayed on the front pages of the
state's dailies until a week before the November 1986 election—
which Clements won by a margin of 56 to 44 percent.

"You have to put this in the context of Karl Rove," said an
Austin political consultant. "Rove equates politics with war. And in
war, you do whatever you have to do in order to win. You take calculated risks in order to win. It's a totally different way of looking
at an election. That doesn't mean he did it. But in war, you do what
you have to to destroy your enemy."

In the spring of 2000, after Rove had destroyed John McCain in
the South Carolina primary and secured the Republican presidential nomination for George W. Bush, he referred to the 1986 bugging in a conversation that nagged at the reporter interviewing him.
Melinda Henneberger wrote in *The New York Times Magazine* that
when she looked into the 1986 bugging, she asked herself if Rove
would "really have gone that far for a client." She described the
bugging as "the weirdest story about Rove-related intrigue." She
initially concluded that Rove would not have done it.

Then she rented *Power*—a movie Rove recommended while she

was working on the story. *Power* is a Sidney Lumet film about a political consultant played by Richard Gere. "I thought of myself as the Gere character," Rove had told Henneberger when he suggested she see the film. "He has the fabulous office and the New York high-rise and he gets paid $25,000 a month by everybody. You got to rent this. It's so unbelievably stupid. He's working for this total schlump, and of course they get the schlump elected governor."

Rove thought the plot was unrealistic because guys like him weed out the schlumps. In the end, they don't get elected. That's not what Henneberger found so fascinating. What struck her as she watched the film was that in the heat of the gubernatorial race, Gere's character discovers his office had been bugged. The film was released in 1986.

She mentioned the coincidence to Rove and he laughed. "Then he stopped laughing and kind of cocked his head. Then he said, 'I don't have any recollection of that.'"

Was Karl Rove directing a writer to a fictitious representation of himself? Or was he so secure in his new position of power that he was reminding this Washington reporter from a national daily that had been unkind to his boss that he was now in charge? So much in charge that he could tease the reporter by alluding to something he had been accused of sixteen years earlier?

What Henneberger called "Rove-related intrigue" about the 1986 office bugging didn't end when the FBI filed its report in 1986. In the aftermath of the discovery of the bug, an FBI agent named Greg Rampton interrogated Clements campaign staffers about the bug. Four years later, in almost perfect synchronicity with the beginning of the 1992 election campaigns, Rove and Rampton were again brought together in Austin, where the FBI agent was working a case.

One of Rampton's contacts was Karl Rove. All of Rampton's targets were Democrats. Two of them would end up in federal prison.

Rove had been quick to grasp the structural weakness in the "plural executive" put in place by the Texas Constitution. If an election to the American presidency is, as Rove would remind reporters ten years later, "fifty separate elections," a race for governor of Texas is six separate elections. The constitution divides the powers associated with a chief executive among the governor, lieutenant governor, attorney general, comptroller, land commissioner, and agriculture commissioner. New York elects a governor. Texas elects a cabinet.

The result of this division in a party whose candidates were accustomed to settling their scores in the primary before going on to defeat weak Republicans were evident to Rove. In 1990, the Democratic Party in Texas was Ann Richards and her consultant and mailing list; Bob Bullock and his consultant and mailing list; Jim Mattox and his consultant and mailing list; Jim Hightower and his consultant and mailing list; and Garry Mauro and his consultant and mailing list.

One of the advantages Rove realized working for a small but growing party was that Karl Rove + Company had the Clements mailing list. The same list Rove started putting together when Bum Bright had hired him to raise money. The same contacts with big Republican funders that Rove used to build his direct mail firm, where Clements was his first client. As Austin consultant Bill Miller saw it, Rove was there first: He knew where the money was in the state's Republican community, and he knew where the voters were. Republican party discipline also helped. The Republicans had an organizing principle: They were out of power and they wanted in. Democrats believe Rove used more than direct mail and smart campaigns to get them in.

Among the stars of the Democrats' Class of 1982, Land Commissioner Garry Mauro was the brash one, always in a hurry. The grandson of Sicilian immigrants, briefly an undersized, walk-on lineman for his beloved Aggies at Texas A&M, he grew up wanting to be the governor of Texas and didn't mean to wait until his hair turned gray. There were other campus politicos of note in College Station in those years—John Sharp, Rick Perry, Henry Cisneros. Mauro figured he was the measure of any of them. He organized Aggies for Bobby Kennedy in the 1968 presidential race and worked for liberal icons Ralph Yarborough and George McGovern.

Mauro had many teachers in the Democratic Party, but none meant as much to him as Bob Bullock. When Bullock won the comptroller's race in 1974, he hired Mauro and made him a senior deputy. He would send Mauro around the state to execute his on-the-spot firings of employees. Mauro didn't have the temperament to bully and hector like his mentor, but employees in the comptroller's office called him "Little Bullock," and he tried to live up to the honor.

After Mauro won the 1982 race for land commissioner, he and Bullock talked by phone almost daily. Cocky as Adonis, Mauro created image problems for himself almost at once. He got creamed, as had Bullock, for overindulging the novelty and luxury of having a state-owned plane at his call. Environmentalists thought he was much too friendly with developers. Mauro put his face on billboards advertising benefits for veterans. And like Bullock, he was tainted by his association in treacherous Duval County with an oil-patch hustler named Clinton Manges, who had long been a source

of money for Democratic candidates. They laughed about the shots
being fired at them, most days.

Then one day Bullock called and said they had to talk, and not
by phone—he was coming over. Bullock drove the short distance
between their buildings, and he came by himself, which was not his
style; he almost always had aides with him. Bullock was not the
kind to be frightened or intimidated by anyone, but as they rode
around central Austin, Mauro could tell that he was badly spooked.
According to Mauro, Bullock said, "Garry, Karl Rove is in league
with a guy in the U.S. attorney's office in San Antonio. He's an FBI
agent named Greg Rampton. Their sole job right now, their mission
in life, is to figure out a way to indict you, me, Jim Mattox, Jim
Hightower, and Ann Richards. They're out to get us all."

Mauro knew Rove slightly. Before Mauro graduated to the state
pool fleet, they had been fellow regulars on Southwest Airlines com-
muter flights between Austin, Dallas, and Houston; rival pols and
consultants saw each other and mingled all the time. Apart from the
land office, Mauro had a dormant law practice with Ed Wendler, a
veteran Democratic consultant. Wendler practiced local politics, as
well as the statewide variety. He had been trying to help unseat a
city council member in the suburb of Round Rock. "There was a
very nice woman involved in that," Wendler recalled. "She was a
Republican, a neighborhood organizer. She called me one day and
said, 'We have this young man, a political consultant, who'd like to
help us. Would you talk to him?' I said, 'Sure, I'll talk to anybody.'
That was my introduction to Karl. We worked together on that.
Every suggestion he made was right on the money. But the thing
that struck me about him was that he was emotionless. All that
counted to him was winning. I told Garry then, 'This guy exists,

and he is a threat.' It wasn't very long before we started hearing about Karl and the FBI agent. Bullock was consumed by that."

In the years Rampton was in Texas, he cut a swath that left several careers and reputations in ruin, and he never went after Republicans. (His first victim had been an ambitious Waco district attorney named Vic Feazell.) Following Bullock's warning, Mauro began to hear from veterans and contributors that an FBI agent was calling them. He told his general counsel at the land office to call Rampton and tell him they'd provide any records he wanted. Mauro thought the trouble had gone away, but in June 1984, as he was preparing to make a speech at the state Democratic convention in Houston, a reporter with leaked information called and asked him to comment on the FBI's subpoena, half an hour earlier, of 70,000 land office documents. Mauro was suspected of overseeing a land appraisal scheme associated with the veterans' programs.

"There were fourteen of them," he recalled of the guys in black. "They showed up first thing in the morning, and we had rows and rows of boxes waiting. They'd demanded that we provide two computers, and they installed their software and started looking. They must not have found much, because by ten o'clock they were gone. Rampton's thesis was that any contribution from a veteran or a developer had to be quid pro quo." Mauro had a two-year-old son; Bullock was the child's godfather. Mauro found himself being thankful his son was too young to read. The press was brutal; Rampton did not always observe the FBI custom of declining comment on an active investigation. Mauro thought he was going to be indicted and hired a top criminal defense lawyer, Gerry Goldstein of San Antonio. In the argot of Texas courthouses, he feared he was about to go off to the big rodeo.

"I saw Rampton one time after that," he said. "I walked out in the hall, and he was just standing there. He handed me his card, and I asked him into my office, and we had a little chat. I never found out what he was doing there. I just assume he was trying to intimidate me."

The federal indictment never came. No charges were ever filed. Nor was Mauro ever cleared. There was just an FBI letter to Goldstein saying vaguely that the investigation was suspended. Mauro served two more terms as land commissioner, refusing to give up his dream of being governor. But those headlines would always be there, ready-made for any opponent's admaker. What was the political damage? Long afterward, Mauro chuckled at the question. "Well, let's just say I was no longer the Boy Wonder."

If Mauro was the boy wonder, Jim Hightower was the *enfant terrible.* By 1990, the folksy Texas Agriculture Commissioner represented a real threat to the Republican Party in Texas—and perhaps even beyond Texas. He had led his party's ticket in 1982 and 1986, winning by 60–40 margins. He had considered, then backed away from, making a run for the seat of one of Rove's star clients: Senator Phil Gramm. Hightower had worked for Ralph Nader in Washington in the 1960s, then joined the staff of liberal Democratic Senator Ralph Yarborough. He had a blue-collar message that combined Nader's pro-consumer politics with Yarborough's fiery populist oratory.

Before Hightower's election in 1982, the agriculture commission had been a sleepy service bureau for Texas farmers and ranchers—with a growing focus on the big agribusiness combines displacing the state's small ranchers and farmers. Hightower had decided that everyone who eats is somehow involved in agriculture and had opened the agency up to consumer advocates, organic farm consultants, a marketing and small-business-development office, a farmworkers outreach program, a regional farmers market program, and environmental analysts who cast a cold eye on pesticides. He had alienated the big ag-chem and pesticide companies, Republican Governor Bill Clements, and the Texas Farm Bureau. He used his office as a pulpit to rail against the Reagan and Bush administrations' class-based politics. He made the political economy the message, made the message clear and understandable to everyone, and punched it up with lines like: "George Bush was born on third base and thinks he hit a triple."

With the domestic policy stage dominated by Republican budgets that favored the rich over the poor, the plunder of the country's savings and loans, and the public's concern about toxic waste dumps and a safe food supply, Hightower's message seemed pitch perfect. He was unapologetic about his embrace of progressive populism, proclaiming, "There's nothing in the middle of the road but yellow stripes and dead armadillos."

In *The Washington Post* David Maraniss was suggesting that Hightower's moment had arrived. The *Post* reporter sang the agriculture commissioner's praises while quoting Hightower quoting singer and songwriter Bob Wills: "The little bee sucks the blossom, but the big bee gets the honey; the little man picks the cotton but the big man gets the money." Hightower was as relentless in his support of the little man picking the cotton as he was in his attack on the "bullies, bankers, and bastards" running the country.

The contentious ag commissioner from Denison, Texas, might as well have painted a target on his back. It required little of a Republican consultant to recognize that Hightower was a problem for the state and national party. It took considerable skill, on the other hand, to realize he could be beaten. Rove set his sights on the target.

To find an opponent for Hightower in the 1990 election, Rove went to the source that had provided him Phil Gramm: the Democratic Party. It was there that he found Rick Perry, an unremarkable two-term Democratic House member from Central Texas. Perry worked a family ranch with his father, was possessed of youthful good looks, and was as conservative as most Republican members of the House. Rove recruited Perry to the other side of the aisle and began to groom him to run against Hightower. His broader target, beyond the one on Hightower's back, was Perry's constituents: rural Democrats. Rove believed at the time that Republicans were getting all the votes they could out of the cities. Texas was an urban state, so the ballot boxes outside the state's cities no longer made an election—but they could swing one. In Perry, still something of an empty suit, Rove saw a candidate who could defeat Hightower and perhaps draw some rural and small-town Democrats in to the Republican Party. Perry was designated as the candidate who would take on Hightower. He could be marketed to the public as a cowboy, an image that still sells in Texas.

"Some political consultants measure their success by the number of clients they have," said Austin political consultant Bill Miller. Rove, he said, measures his success by the races he wins. Miller also described Rove as the most focused, disciplined, and organized consultant he had ever worked with or against.

Texas Democrats were not prepared for the political campaign Karl Rove could put in the field. Rove raised more than $3 million to sell the name of Rick Perry while tarnishing the name of Jim Hightower. Perry's campaign office established a press presence, putting out scores of press releases in a format similar to wire-service dispatches.

Hightower faced another problem in the campaign. Greg Ramp-ton, the same FBI agent who had been digging around the offices of Garry Mauro and Bob Bullock, had turned his sights on Hightower. In the summer before the general election, while Rove was at a fundraiser in Washington, he announced that Hightower was under investigation and that indictments would be handed down. Hightower cried foul: The U.S. Department of Justice had made no such announcement. Yet the political consultant for his opponent was announcing it to reporters in Washington.

The money Rove raised through direct mail and high-dollar fundraising events paid for the television spots that made Rick Perry a household face in Texas—and Hightower's name synonymous with corruption. And with liberalism. Television ads claimed "Mr. Hightower was under investigation by the F.B.I.," and asked if he was "too liberal for Texas" because he had supported the presidential campaign of Jesse Jackson. Hightower's modest budget confined his message—and his attempts to respond to Rove—to radio spots.

Tracking polls followed Rove's targeted ad campaigns, measuring their success. Democrats, turned on by a governor's race that pitted Ann Richards against West Texas rancher and banker Clayton Williams, were giving their money not to Hightower but to Richards, who was known to be in a tight race. By the weekend before the election, though, independent pollsters knew what the Perry campaign's internal pollsters already had in hand: The seventeen-to-twenty-point lead Hightower had enjoyed was gone and the race was a dead heat.

In the weekend before the election, Perry ran newspaper ads that had Hightower burning flags and shaking hands with Jesse Jackson.

(He was innocent of the former and guilty of the latter.) Another ad was built over clipped headlines that referred to corruption within the Texas Department of Agriculture. The Perry campaign even put out a press release when Hightower carelessly cut off the tip of his finger with a power mower.

The ag commissioner who had won more than 60 percent of the vote in two previous elections lost his bid for a third term by 51 to 49. For a down-ballot statewide office, Rove had put together a campaign with all the intensity and sophistication (and negative campaigning) associated with a senatorial or gubernatorial race. Jim Hightower was left trying to explain how someone with his national following could lose to a newcomer like Rick Perry. He was philosophical about it. Politics, he said, pumped you up until you strutted around like a peacock. "Today," he said, "I stand before you a feather duster."

Although Rove is often described as a "take no prisoners" campaigner, this campaign was an exception. Two years after the election, three of Hightower's assistants were indicted, convicted, and sentenced to short terms in federal prison. They had misused department funds and raised campaign money from agency clients. The federal judge who sentenced them, Sam Sparks (an appointee of President George H. W. Bush), observed that the ag department employees had broken the law. But he was bothered by the fact that they had inherited a corrupt system that had been in place in the Department of Agriculture long before Hightower was elected, and perhaps also by the fact of his presiding over a politically driven prosecution. The sentence he handed down was so light that he was scolded by the U.S. Court of Appeals for the Fifth Circuit for violating federal sentencing guidelines.

It wasn't until after the fact that the connection between Rampton and Rove was established. In March 1991 Rove was summoned to appear before the Texas Senate's Nominations Committee. The format was as familiar as a C-SPAN capitol news feed. The witness is sworn in and faces his inquisitors sitting on an elevated dais. It's the perfect setting for what an East Texas senator once described as "a ritual ass whipping." On this occasion, Rove was going to get one. Governor Bill Clements had nominated him to the East Texas State University's board of regents. The appointment had gone unconfirmed and Clements had since been succeeded by Democrat Ann Richards.

A Democratic senator from the Hill Country began with questions about the bugging of Rove's office while he was directing the Clements campaign for governor in 1986. Then the questioning abruptly turned in another direction. "How long have you known an FBI agent by the name of Greg Rampton?" Rove was asked. Caught off guard, Rove responded much as Bill Clinton did when asked about his relationship with Monica Lewinsky. "Ah, Senator, it depends. Would you define 'know' for me?"

The senator pressed on, determined that "know" could be defined in the context of Rove's relationship with the FBI agent. "Ah, I know, I would not recognize Greg if he walked in the door. We have talked on the phone a var. . . —a number of times. Ah, and he has visited me in my office once or twice. But we do not have a social or personal relationship whatsoever."

The senator kept boring, pressing Rove about the agent who four years earlier had investigated the bugging of his office. But this wasn't about the bugging of Rove's Austin office. It was about Rove's 1990 Washington announcement of the FBI investigation of the Texas Department of Agriculture—at a moment when it could most harm Hightower's campaign.

Rove's only defense was to inform the senator that his characterization of what had happened in Washington was incorrect. The senator had asked Rove if he had issued a news release. "We did not issue a news release," Rove said. "I talked to a member of the press." Rove said the story had already been reported in the *Dallas Morning News.*

The Democratic senator pressed Rove for dates on his contacts with Rampton and Rove admitted they had indeed spoken—in June or July 1990, in October 1990, and then early in 1991. The information came too late to help Hightower. He could get mad but he couldn't get even.

Republicans seized upon Perry's election as agriculture commissioner as the advent of a new approach to electoral politics. Ag commissioner's races had been dull affairs run on the ground in what remained of the good-ol'-boy courthouse network that helped Lyndon Johnson steal a U.S. Senate race in 1948. Rove had elevated the process and made of it a sophisticated multimedia campaign that happened simultaneously in every one of the state's media markets. In doing so, he had taken a smart, ambitious popular statewide official and "drove up his negatives," replacing him with a rural legislator who had achieved nothing of great distiction in two terms in the state house.

He was now free to move on to another member of the Class of '82 dream team that was supposed to dominate the state's politics for twenty years.

4

The End of Democratic Texas

George Herbert Walker Bush couldn't be denied the 1988 Republican nomination, but the vice president was not perceived as a shoo-in candidate for the general election. The favored Democrat, Colorado senator Gary Hart, self-destructed extravagantly and early, going off on a yacht with a groupie and then daring the press to scrutinize his sex and married life. The governor of Massachusetts, Michael Dukakis, took advantage of Hart's stumble and captured the nomination. In the run-up to the conventions, the Democrats wanted to undercut Bush's strength in Texas as much as they could, and the Texas Class of 1982 still had currency in the national party. Texas Democrats jockeyed to get in the limelight at the convention. Jim Hightower, who was then harboring notions of a populist challenge to right-wing Senator Phil Gramm, hoped that he might be given prime time for a funny, rousing, give-'em-hell speech, but the Dukakis team wanted to energize feminist voters, and in the fading art of political oratory, Ann Richards was as good as anyone the Democrats had. The Texas state treasurer was given the keynote at the convention, and by the time she was through, she was a national sensation.

Provided drafts by the party's big-name speechwriters in the frantic preparation for her speech, Richards closed her eyes and pushed away the pages like they were spoiled food. With time running out, she started talking it through with the only speechwriter she'd ever used, Austin's Suzanne Coleman. Finally the cameras came on, the anchormen paused, the lights came up, and Richards appeared, stunning in her mane of silver hair and sleek, blue dress. "Twelve years ago," she began, "Barbara Jordan, another Texas woman, made the keynote address to this convention, and two women in 160 years is about par for the course. But if you give us a chance, we can perform. After all, Ginger Rogers did everything that Fred Astaire did. She just did it backwards and in high heels!" In half a dozen breaths she had called up civil rights, reminded her audience of the moral high ground that Jordan had held during the Watergate hearings, and inspired the hopes and pride of Democratic women; the crowd was swept up, roaring.

Richards talked about sitting on a pallet with her small granddaughter and thinking about what the future in this country ought to hold for her. But her language was barbed as well. She attacked the Republican vice president with down-home mockery and ridicule, tearing into one Bush policy by saying "That old dog won't hunt." But the speech would be best remembered for her grinning delivery of one tart line: "Poor George. He can't help it. He was born with a silver foot in his mouth!"

Unfortunately, few people would be able to recall what Dukakis said when he took his turn at the podium to accept his party's nomination. Even so, the Dukakis team did make one more astute move, naming Texas' senior U.S. senator, Lloyd Bentsen, as the candidate's running mate. Bentsen was the man who had defeated George Bush in the 1970 Senate race, and he played tennis regularly with Bush's most trusted adviser, James Baker. "Interesting," Bush responded when told the news. "That's interesting."

The Bush team stumbled when it came time to select a running mate. The conventional wisdom was that Indiana Senator Dan Quayle was chosen because he was young and attractive—and therefore appealing to women and to younger voters. But "lightweight" was the press epithet that at once caught hold.

At the Republican convention the GOP's most skillful speechwriter, Peggy Noonan, got the speech of his life out of Bush. Nobody knew what Bush meant by a thousand points of light, but he seemed to imagine and believe in them, and he at last emerged from the shadow of Ronald Reagan as his own man. Dukakis' seventeen-point lead in the polls evaporated, and the rout was on. In the debates, the Democratic nominee proved to be his own worst enemy. When Dukakis, who opposed the death penalty, was asked how he'd feel if someone raped and murdered his wife, he gave a bland, unemotional answer that confirmed his image as a cold fish. The sole bright spot for the Democrats was the performance of Lloyd Bentsen. He embarrassed Quayle in their debate when, in the context of youth, the Republican likened himself to John F. Kennedy. Bentsen was ready for that one. "Senator, I served with Jack Kennedy," he replied. "I knew Jack Kennedy. Jack Kennedy was a friend of mine. Senator, you're no Jack Kennedy."

But the Democratic glee over Bentsen's rhetorical victory was short-lived. Not long after, Dukakis was traveling in Texas, where he asked his convention keynote speaker to fly with him. He asked Richards how she thought the campaign was going. She responded by yelling, "*What* campaign?" and lighting into him in characteristic fashion. They did not communicate closely after that.

What campaign, indeed. While Dukakis micromanaged his campaign into the answer to a Trivial Pursuit question, the Bush campaign was rampaging across the nation under the direction of Rove's old buddy Lee Atwater.

At the outset of the campaign Bush had called his children to Houston to meet the campaign staff. It was there that Atwater found himself confronted by the vice president's curly-haired eldest son, who was not much older than the boy-wonder strategist. George W. Bush had one question for Atwater: "How can we trust you?"

Atwater, taken aback, was speechless.

"Listen, pal," the son continued in his slightly acidic drawl, "if you go to war for our family, we want you completely on our side. We love George Bush, and you better bust your ass for him."

Atwater busted ass for George Bush, and as the campaign wore on he and George W. could increasingly be found in each other's vicinity, laughing and hooting over some shared joke. It was the apotheosis of Atwater's career. Rove's old friend from the College Republicans of the seventies changed the culture of presidential politics by putting a face—especially a mouth—on the consultant. As he saw it, his job was to take flak aimed for the candidate and keep up an outrageous, distracting patter. (James Carville, among others, owes a great debt to Lee Atwater for his celebrity status.) But Atwater was also a disciple of Richard Nixon's gospel of dirty tricks. Atwater dug up the story of a murderer named Willie Horton, who had committed rape and assault while on furlough from a Massachusetts prison, and in ads that clanged like cellblock doors made the name synonymous with Dukakis' record. Atwater's attack ads were criticized as racist, but that charge was harder to pin on George Bush, who maintained a discreet distance from the ads themselves (which were produced by an independent advocacy group). Atwater also had great fun with Dukakis' description of his state's suddenly faltering economy as "the Massachusetts Miracle," and Bush was sent out on a watercraft to cluck at all the dreadful pollution in Boston Harbor. The final nail in the coffin, though, was Atwater's interception of a videotape that showed Dukakis going for a photo-op spin in a tank, his foolish grin and ill-fitting helmet conveying the acuity of a turtle. Atwater didn't really need to run the campaign like General Sherman's march to the sea, but that was his style, and by election day Dukakis the politician had been reduced to ashes.

Karl Rove's closeness to Atwater and the elder Bush's growing fondness for him gave him a limited but important role in the campaign: His reputation, once more, was for painstaking data assembly and effective direct mail.

In the sweep, Bush carried Texas easily. He was about to become the most powerful man in the world; he would preside over the fall of the Iron Curtain and the breakup of the Soviet Union. Under his watch America at last won the cold war, and then crushed the supposed Iraqi might of Saddam Hussein. Yet back in Texas, the 1988 convention speech had made Ann Richards the political darling of the season. First the lieutenant governor, Bill Hobby, and then the telegenic mayor of San Antonio, Henry Cisneros, decided to get out of the way for whatever race she chose in 1990.

The attorney general, Jim Mattox, was another member of the Democratic class of '82, and Richards had been a close ally when he was an anti-establishment state representative and congressman from Dallas. Richards' husband, David, from whom she was now separated, was a labor and civil rights lawyer and had come into the government fold for the first time to direct litigation for Mattox. The attorney general's strong-arm fundraising got him indicted, but a state jury acquitted Mattox, and he immediately started huffing and puffing that no one had better get between him and the governor's mansion.

Richards ignored him. She talked longingly of running for lieutenant governor, the office that controls all Senate appointments and legislation through presiding over the Senate. But she had to make a living. The Texas constitution provided that the lieutenant governor received a salary of just $7,200 a year, the same as everyone else in the state legislature. Salaries in the executive branch, on the other hand, were livable, if not generous, and Richards needed a regular paycheck; she wasn't wealthy. Just as significantly, the more she talked to her core supporters, the more she realized the depth of their feeling. It was time for a woman governor, they believed, and she was the one. They expected her to run.

Richards kicked off her 1990 campaign by chartering a yacht and making a port-by-port tour of the long Texas coast. Local officials, activists, and business people came aboard during the days and briefed her on issues as capitol bureau reporters dozed, and the imagery of a yacht might easily have turned on her. But compared to Mattox's angry demeanor, it was a media feast. On free television all over the state, she was seen piloting the craft as dolphins leaped and cavorted in her wake.

Meanwhile, the scutwork of the campaign was being done in her campaign office in Austin, which was as seedy, disordered, and down-and-dirty as that of any of the other Democrats. One of her campaign managers was the young consultant Mark McKinnon, who was smooth, literate, and patient with the caustic outbursts she tended to unleash when she got tired. But the most impassioned and skillful worker in the Richards campaign was a young state legislator named Lena Guerrero. Demographics were changing Texas politics as much as anything Democrats or Republicans had done; the time was soon coming when Hispanics would be the state's most numerous ethnic group. Karl Rove and other astute Republicans knew they had better be ready to ride that wave of change. Guerrero personified the Democrats' determination to make sure this particular power base continued to vote Democratic. The youthful state rep was the best utility player on the party's farm team, an aggressive campaigner who had clawed her way into the statehouse when she was twenty-five and barely out of the University of Texas. She had proved to be a capable legislator, revealing herself as a natural floor tactician, someone who could muscle votes into place and hold them there when they threatened to slip away. And she was completely and genuinely bilingual and bicultural.

Her political résumé was almost too good to be true and offered the outline of a dramatic American success story. Born in the Lower Rio Grande Valley, as a child she had worked as a migrant farmworker, following the harvest season with her family. She left the poor, dusty Mission Acres *colonia* to attend the University of Texas, where she graduated with a degree in communications and a Phi Beta Kappa key.

Karl Rove read all this carefully.

In those days, the Texas AFL-CIO convention was tantamount to a Democratic caucus. Jim Mattox expected labor to come through for him with an endorsement, for he had been their champion for years, but Richards wasn't going to let him walk away without a tussle. The Austin convention rapidly turned into a heated floor fight between the Mattox and Richards camps as they maneuvered for support from the assembled delegates. Few people in that hall had ever seen a cell phone before, but Guerrero was all over the hall with one, barking orders at her colleagues, sweet-talking crusty old refinery and dock workers, making Mattox aides so angry some observers wondered when she was going to get punched. It was a phenomenal performance. Labor chose to remain neutral in the Democratic race, a crucial setback for Mattox and a win for Richards.

Guerrero did everything but throw her body in front of a truck to deny Mattox the Democratic nomination. One reporter observed that Richards owed her improved chances to the resilience of Guerrero's bladder, wondering, "Does she ever have to pee? She never left the floor. She was out there with that portable phone all day."

As other constituent groups met to consider who they would endorse in the campaign, Guerrero (whose surname in English means "warrior") would attend to spar on Richards' behalf. At the Mexican-American Democrats convention in Corpus Christi, Guerrero stood *frente a frente* with Mattox, staring down an opponent who had all the advantages of height, weight, and gender.

Far behind in the polls, Mattox went negative, as everyone expected he would. He jumped on Richards' rowdy past and social ties to Austin musicians and hippies. He accused her of using marijuana and cocaine, and the press did not give Richards the same pass it would later grant George W. Bush when the same subject came up. "Answer the question! Answer the question!" reporters screamed at Richards as she walked out of one debate. Richards and many of her supporters thought the race was over. Former governor Mark White jumped into the contest, hoping for a comeback, and Richards' backers began to fear that she might not even make the run-off.

But Richards survived the primary, and the run-off with Mattox, though she was a battered candidate. A Democratic primary was often described—especially by Rove and other Republicans—as the last place in Texas where liberals could have their way. The Texas electorate was no less conservative just because Ann Richards had won the nomination. Knowing this, Richards replaced Mark McKinnon's campaign team with one headed by her old friend and chief of staff at the treasury, Mary Beth Rogers, and she prepared to take on the Republican candidate, oilman and rancher Clayton Williams.

Clayton Williams was a true outsider. He was a West Texas Aggie with money to burn, but unlike Bill Clements he didn't pay much attention to advice from young folks who made their living in politics. In the Republican primary, he had overwhelmed a Dallas attorney named Tom Luce, the favorite of the country club crowd, and Kent Hance, the West Texan who had beaten George W. Bush in the 1978 congressional race and then switched parties to get in step with Ronald Reagan. Hance was Rove's client in the race and would later recall how bad Rove felt about losing the race. "He does not take losing easily," Hance said. "We got outspent by Clayton Williams five-to-one. The one thing I liked best about Rove: It became obvious it was going to be a miracle if we won, but he stayed focused and committed. He stayed hitched."

Clements seemed to have run for another term in 1986 because he was ornery and vain and just wanted to get even with Mark White. Under Texas law he could have sought a third term, but he had accomplished what he set out to do. Poor health and the resulting physical discomfort had become bothersome to him, and as a regent of Southern Methodist University, he had let himself get sucked into a hush-money scandal involving football players, coaches, and big-shot Dallas alumni. At the time, the SMU Mustangs boasted future NFL great Eric Dickerson and had played two fine seasons that stirred memories of Doak Walker and Dandy Don Meredith, but the payoffs that Clements admitted to sanctioning were so outrageous that the NCAA imposed the "death penalty" for the first time, canceling all football scholarships and kicking the school out of intercollegiate competition for a season. From afar, the football recruiting scandal—which ultimately involved all the major schools in the state but one—looked like an exotic barn dance of Texans who had too much money and too little to think about. But within the state it was a huge story. Clements still had plenty of juice and vigor, but it was time for him to head for the sidelines of GOP politics.

Karl Rove's focus in the 1990 elections was Rick Perry, whose campaign against Jim Hightower would successfully dethrone this prominent member of the Class of '82. Another significant change of regime was occurring in the office of the lieutenant governor. Bill Hobby was retiring, and after sixteen years as comptroller, Bob Bullock had decided that he wanted to cap his career by ascending to the powerful lieutenant governor's office. To a much greater entent than the other Democrats running statewide that year, Bullock had friends and donors in both parties, in addition to a reputation that would cause any would-be challenger to think twice. He drew only token Republican opposition.

In the governor's race, Clayton Williams seemed to think that he could just spit and grin and good-ol'-boy his way into office. And he might have. There were a lot of fellow good ol' boys in Texas.

Richards' own polls had her twenty points down at Labor Day. But Williams' uncalculated crudeness made Bill Clements look like a French dancing instructor by comparison. When he encountered Richards at their debate, the old cowboy refused to shake Richards' hand, an unchivalrous moment caught on film and reproduced on televisions across the state. He said he was going to "head her and hoof her," an expression rodeo calf ropers use to describe roping and tying a calf. He told reporters visiting his ranch a crude joke about the thunderstorm that was descending on them: Bad weather, he said, is like rape. "You can't do anything about it, so you might as well lay back and enjoy it." As the campaign came down to the wire, he casually allowed as how one year he hadn't had to pay any federal income taxes.

Early in the afternoon on election day, anticipation and excitement among the Democrats began to race through Austin. One of the party stalwarts was a former county judge from West Texas named Bill Young. He said he always got a haircut on election day, and his barber was the most accurate pollster he knew. Young said he came out of the shop convinced that Jim Hightower was in big trouble, but his barber also said that he couldn't bring himself to vote for Williams: "I looked at that ballot, and the face of that ignorant son of a bitch just swum up at me," he said. Young's barber wasn't alone. Middle-class wives and mothers who had never voted for a Democrat in their lives were thronging to vote for Richards.

The two candidates' election-night parties could have been scripted by a Democratic consultant. Williams' thwarted victory celebration was an invitation-only affair, and as the grim results of the day's voting trickled in, the roomful of Williams' big-money, big-hat, big-hair supporters became noticeably boisterous and inebriated. By the time the candidate appeared onstage to attempt a concession speech, he had trouble making himself heard above the crowd that had ostensibly gathered on his behalf. When he spoke Richards' name, a torrent of catcalls and shouted slurs drowned him out, and he had to raise his hands quiet the room, to no avail. "Now . . now . . you *owe me that courtesy,*" he hissed, visibly angry. The effect was striking: a roomful of millionaire yahoos who wouldn't even let their own candidate speak. The good-ol'-boy system was breaking down, live, on camera, and only the caterers would know how ugly it had really gotten.

Across town, at the Richards party, euphoria was in the air, and it was catching. Richards' celebration was open to anybody who wanted to walk in off the street, and as the poll results swept across Austin, people were getting up off their couches and going downtown to help celebrate the victory. Grizzled political veterans and true-believer campaign workers mixed with supporters who had never thought of themselves as being particularly political before. Over and over the same remark was heard: "I can't believe Ann won." That was how she was referred to, even by people who had never seen her in person before: *Ann.* It was as though everyone in the room was celebrating the triumph of a personal friend, and her appearance was greeted with unrestrained displays of emotion.

The larger significance wasn't lost on the grizzled vets nursing their drinks in the back of the room watching the Richard's celebration. A woman who had made her political career with a tongue-lashing of President Bush had been elected governor of Texas. When Williams' West Texas supporters descended on Austin restaurants the next day for pricey and joyless lunches, resentment of the capital and everything it stood for was etched plainly on their faces.

In the closing weeks Richards had taken up a refrain that when she won, she was going to lead a people's march up Austin's Congress Avenue—the people were going to take the government back. Inauguration Day in January 1991 was clear, cold, and blustery. Hundreds of supporters gathered that morning at the Town Lake bridge, and with Richards in the lead and Lena Guerrero close by her side, in blue jeans and sneakers and windbreakers they came up the broad street laughing, hollering, arm in arm. In offices above the ground level, businessmen could be seen at the windows, smiling at the spectacle, charitable for the moment. Few people heard Richards' inauguration speech on the Capitol steps, because of press helicopters hovering close overhead. After it was over, a group of her new aides ran to the Sam Houston Building to occupy their offices. The elevator doors opened on a group of well-groomed white men in suits, all carrying briefcases. They absorbed the rabble's appearance and blanched. They cut their eyes and slipped through without speaking. They were the outgoing staff of Governor Bill Clements, people who were used to getting orders—unofficially, of course—from Karl Rove.

The suburban women who would be described as soccer moms a few election cycles later had thronged to the polls to vote for the outspoken grandmother who promised a government as open to women as it had been to men. "The rooster crows, but the hen delivers," Richards had said. In her political appointments, she promised to award talent, intelligence, and loyalty, and one of her most talented, smart, and loyal lieutenants was Lena Guerrero. "Lena Guerrero won the primary for Ann Richards," said state legislator Irma Rangel, a savvy South Texas lawyer who easily shifts from English to Spanish. She then punctuated her declaration: "Pues, así es." Well, so it is.

Richards repaid Guerrero when a seat opened up on the Texas

Railroad Commission, appointing her to fill out the remainder of the departing commissioner's term. The post may sound like a bureaucratic backwater, but it carries real power, and has long served emerging Texas candidates as a springboard to higher office. The state's three railroad commissioners regulate railroads, trucking, oil, and natural gas. But it's the oil and gas regulation that put the commission on the map. Years earlier, a group of oil-rich countries had used the Railroad Commission as a model to form their own price-control cabal—today known by the acronym OPEC.

The appointment was more than a political payback. Of course Richards was rewarding Guerrero for her talent, intelligence, and loyalty. But she also perceived that Guerrero was ambitious and tough enough to run for statewide office. ("They're going to pick through your innards when you run," Richards warned her.) With President George Bush, a nominal Texan, at the top of the ticket in 1992, voters might well cast straight-party ballots that started with the Republican presidential candidate and carried down-ballot to the Republican candidate for justice of the peace. Richards saw Guerrero as a firewall who could stop voters from pulling that straight-party lever—and as a vote-driver in cities on the Texas-Mexico border and in the growing Hispanic communities in Houston, Fort Worth, and Dallas.

Guerrero moved into the offices of what had been a three-man agency and became the Commission's good ol' girl. She mastered arcane oil and gas regulation and traveled the state visiting local Railroad Commission offices. She connected with funders (one of the advantages of holding statewide office) and prepared to campaign to retain her seat on the Commission in 1992. Guerrero had no opposition for the office in the Democratic primary, and when the campaign for the general election began, she was trailed by a Republican lawyer who had run the Minerals Management Agency for President Bush. In little time she had moved from *Texas Monthly*'s "Top Ten Legislators" list to *USA Today*'s list of women to watch as possible future presidential contenders.

Ann Richards had begun her 1988 Democratic convention speech with the line: "Buenas noches, mis amigos." At the 1992 convention in New York, delegates heard the same line with a far more authentic accent. Guerrero wasn't a big enough star to get the keynote, but Richards helped her secure a primetime speaking slot. Guerrero delivered a pitch-perfect *del barrio salí yo* speech that read like a treatment for an Edwards James Olmos miniseries. If "hope flutters on broken wings" was bad poetics and she had to compete with baseball's All-Star Game, Lena was no less a star.

But not for long.

While political reporters in Austin were calling the race for Guerrero, Rove was quietly working to ensure that the speech in Madison Square Garden was the end of her political career. Before her name was even listed on the program for the Democratic National Convention, he had received a call from the spouse of one of his clients, who told Rove that according to information obtained from a University of Texas alumni group, Guerrero was not a graduate. Student transcripts are not public records, but it's often impossible to keep them private. *The New Yorker*, after all, informed the world in 2000 that George W. Bush was a C student at Yale. But at least Bush graduated. Guerrero did not. Nor was she a C student. In fact, the number of Cs, incompletes, and Fs on her transcript dropped a broad hint to Rove that she had never been inducted into Phi Beta Kappa, either. As did the fact that Phi Beta

Kappa keys are awarded only to arts and science graduates, not to graduates of the College of Communications.

Once the transcript was delivered to Rove, there was little doubt that it would become part of the public record. Rove was ever the colleague and disciple of Lee Atwater, who had elevated smear tactics to an art form. Atwater had died in 1991 of a brain tumor (he was only forty years old), but his approach to politics lived on through Rove. And there was little imagination required here; an Atwater intern could have done this deal. But not as skillfully as Karl Rove. Ann Richards' "New Texas" was a place (or at least a concept) where gender-blind meritocracy would replace the good ol' boys' bureaucracy. Fresh new faces would bring new ideas to government. The New Texas had captured the imagination of voters. Now its brightest young star was a fraud who had lied about her degree and claimed academic honors she never earned.

If "location, location, and location" sells real estate, "timing, timing, and timing" wins elections.

Rove waited. He waited until after the Democratic primary, when Guerrero was the only viable Democratic candidate. He waited until after Guerrero delivered the commencement speech at Texas A&M University, and told students: "I remember well my own commencement." He waited until after the Democratic convention, when Guerrero's profile was higher than it had ever been. And he waited until after his own candidate for the Railroad Commission, Barry Williamson, gave his midday speech to the Republican National Convention.

When a reporter from the *Dallas Morning News* called and asked Guerrero about her degree, she claimed there was an error and she would check with the university. In fact, she was buying enough time to release the information herself—a practice political consultants call "inoculating" a story. Days of bad political theater and partial corrections followed. The three credits Guerrero lacked became nineteen. More details trickled out. The star legislator had failed a course on the Texas Legislature. The Latina role model had failed a course on Mexican Americans in the Southwest.

"Karl had Lena's transcript," said an Austin political consultant. "But he held it until the right moment. The perfect moment. Then he screwed her."

Guerrero tried to redeem herself by resigning from the Commission so she would face Williamson as a candidate and not an incumbent. She had made a mistake but had done a good job in the Legislature and on the Railroad Commission. She would "let the voters decide."

They did. Williamson won by a thirteen-point spread. He even beat Guerrero in South Texas, where the majority of registered voters are Hispanic.

"The First Chink in Richards' Armor" was the *Houston Chronicle*'s headline on Guerrero's loss. In her first two years in office, Richards had seemed invulnerable. The collapse of her protégée altered that image.

It was a prelude to November 1994.

Ann Richards' press secretary was a tall, wry ex-political beat reporter named Bill Cryer. An aide to Bob Bullock had first ushered Cryer out of the press and into the fold of politics, but initially he had landed among the Republicans, getting a job in the 1982 re-election campaign of Governor Bill Clements, and for three months he worked elbow-to-elbow with Karl Rove. Cryer greatly enjoyed the collegiality in the campaign office, and coming from a newspaper press room, he couldn't believe the digs. "They had so much money," Cryer reminisced. "The office was in a swank Austin highrise, and anytime we needed to go anywhere, some rich guy had a plane waiting at the airport. Karl struck me as the consummate Young Republican. Well-spoken and funny—a great story-teller. They were all like that. Karl was the direct-mail whiz, but he was enraptured by what they were learning to do with computers. They were kids with new toys."

The Democrats also had computers, of course. Cryer recalled the election day that turned into a nightmare for Clements and his young hard chargers. "The exit polls started looking shaky, and it was raining hard over in East Texas. We got a call that blacks and refinery workers were standing in line outside the polls in a downpour. Something was happening out there, and it did not bode well for the governor. Karl and the others were blindsided; they didn't see it coming. They felt terrible for the old man, wondered how they'd let him down and all that, but they were pros. Karl in particular had this gallows humor about it all. That was the end of my dalliance with the Republicans. Ann Richards won the race for treasurer, and she hired me to do the press there. When that was announced Karl sent me a nice short note, and as time went by, and she was elected governor, he and I corresponded occasionally. His notes were always hand-written on very classy stationery. Some little anecdote, thought for the day. He could be a very charming fellow. What's the word for him in those days? Puckish. He had a puckish sense of humor."

Rove was more than mischievous in the way he went after Mark White, Jim Hightower, and Garry Mauro, but he was careful about playing hardball with the head of the Class of '82. Richards' election as a Democrat in Texas might have been a demographic fluke and beneficiary of a poor Republican candidate, but she was a popular governor and much-admired person. After the 1992 presidential election, which sent George Bush home to Texas, the former president's eldest son began testing the waters, just thinking about running against her. A Republican women's group in Dallas asked George W. Bush to participate in a comedy skit. A Republican consultant who was helping the women with the event told *The New York Times* that he got a stern call from Rove: "He said Bush would make fun of himself, his mother or whatever," he recalled, "but he would not under any circumstances make fun of Ann Richards and would appear only on that condition. It's a year out! Bush hasn't even said he's running. This is a skit for the faithful. But Karl has decided that they're not going to run against Ann's personality, because she has a great personality, so he's on the phone, all serious."

Rove knew the Democrats still had a formidable team. Through election or appointment, they controlled all but two of the state agencies. They had strong majorities in both chambers of the legislature, an able house speaker and small-town champion in the Panhandle's Pete Laney, and, above all, in the state's most powerful office, the lieutenant governor, Bob Bullock.

Bullock had been leery of Rove since the FBI investigations of the 1980s, but through intermediaries Bullock was approachable and could be flattered. He had never been a party stalwart, except in the rare times he thought it was in his self-interest to be. Neither had Bullock ever been tempted to get much involved in national politics. In the run-up to the 1994 elections, Republicans began to lay the groundwork for an accommodation with Bullock, giving him a freer hand in the Senate. Rove knew that if an adversary could be co-opted, he didn't have to be defeated.

Richards' relationship with Bullock was long, complicated, and testy. They had been friends, allies, and drinking partners, before they realized, about the same time, that their lives were out of control and went off to "drunk school," as Bullock put it. But they were rivals, too. Richards never fully trusted her lieutenant governor—and especially his staff—and in her office she used to laugh about how he tried to manipulate her. Richards came in as governors often did, promising that she was going to follow her best instincts and advice, let the dice roll, and not worry about getting reelected. That bravado was thrown out at once. She had to lead a conservative state while tamping down her reputation and past history as a liberal. She was photographed dove-hunting in the Panhandle so she could push through legislative priorities like drug treatment programs in the prisons. As governor she continually had to play to Texans' comfort level, and that became difficult, for unlike Bullock she enjoyed being a national celebrity.

A *Houston Chronicle* dispatch from a party hosted by Richards at the 1992 Democratic National Convention in New York began, "You would have thought it was a movie premiere." Among Richards' 1,200 invitees were Dan Rather, Bob Strauss, Barbara Jordan, and Hillary Clinton; Bill Cosby sent her fifty yellow roses. "In the flash of a rose-colored evening suit and sparkling rose-colored earrings," the reporter enthused, "the governor dashed back into The Supper Club, only to emerge once again hand-in-hand with Clinton for the photo opportunity of the night."

After the 1992 election, George W. Bush was mystified at how his father's presidency had just slipped away. How could you win a

war and have a 90 percent approval rating and in just a few months
get bounced back to Houston? George W. could never really admit
that Bill Clinton beat his dad. The damage, he thought, had been
done by Pat Buchanan, nipping away at the president in New
Hampshire and then making that scary and offensive speech at the
GOP convention, and then by Ross Perot piling on. George H. W.
Bush carried Texas in 1992, but the Democrats pinned him down
and made him spend unplanned millions to avoid the embarrassment of losing his home state. "The death of a thousand cuts," the
son would say, stretching his mouth and shaking his head. For the
sake of his dad and the pride of the family, he wanted to get even.

After his father's crushing loss, George W. Bush, by now the
managing partner of the Texas Rangers baseball team, distracted
himself by training to run a marathon, averaging under nine minutes a mile. This was a guy, Rove saw, with tremendous discipline
and energy. Rove had had a good run in Texas himself. He'd picked
Rick Perry as a presentable candidate who knocked Hightower off
his high horse as agriculture commissioner, and in the same year got
Kay Bailey Hutchison, an ex-University of Texas cheerleader and
former television reporter, to run for the treasurer's office vacated
by Richards. But those were down-ballot races, and Rove was past
forty now. If he was going to become a bigger player—even a
national player—and really know power, this was his chance.
George W. Bush was his star.

When Bush announced that he was going to challenge Richards in
the 1994 race, she had a 70 percent approval rating—and yet at the
very start, polls had him only eight points down. "If his name was

George Smith," Richards aides grew fond of saying, "nobody would take him seriously." But this was actually a tremendous gift to his campaign manager—first, George W. *was* George W. Bush, with national name recognition, and second, he was constantly being underestimated. Rove also had run a governor's office and had a mind for policy, as well as political ideology. He saw not only that issues determined electoral outcomes, but that, because of this, the campaign was never-ending. Rove was a master at keeping his candidates "on-message." At the outset, he persuaded Bush to run on four issues: juvenile justice, improvement of public education, relief from property taxes, and tort reform—the last a euphemism for cutting the legal legs out from under plaintiffs' trial lawyers, who were among the Democratic Party's largest contributors. Over and over, Bush made the same pitch. Rove kept him on a continual circuit of small and mid-sized towns, where he visited courthouses and talked to small radio stations and weekly newspapers, his Midland drawl tuned to perfection. While Richards hobnobbed with Cybill Shepherd and Lily Tomlin, her challenger would run into Dallas Cowboy great Roger Staubach, a devout Republican, and joke with the quarterback: "Hey, Roger, I want you and Nolan Ryan"—recently retired from the Rangers' pitching staff—"to campaign with me in the fall. We'll call it the Old Farts' Tour."

Message was everything with Rove. And Bush was notoriously bad when speaking on his feet. At one point early in the campaign when Bush began to deviate from his script, Rove pulled him off the campaign trail for a brief retreat in the seclusion of East Texas. "All we'd heard about was Bush the playboy," said Bill Cryer. "Undisciplined in his personal life. We thought he'd get out there and start popping off, and the press would just cream him. But Karl had him almost on this mantra—Governor Richards called him a windup doll. And Karl very effectively kept him insulated from the press. Any dealing he had with a reporter was on a personal level." One such reporter was Ken Herman, the beat reporter for the *Austin American-Statesman*. Herman had won a Pulitzer as a small-town investigative reporter, and he went after Bush the candidate on occasion. But he loved baseball, and appreciated a funny story. Bush knew how to get him laughing. He would call Herman at home and ask him for advice on what to do with a major league baseball player. The disarming charm was hard to resist.

Apart from the personal qualities a politician brings to the governor's office in Texas, his or her greatest power lies in making appointments. "The Lena Guerrero episode hurt us more than anything," Cryer believed. "Here was a governor who said she was going to make a point of naming women and ethnic minorities to these powerful positions, and she picks one who's unqualified, and lies about it. That was really when we began to feel the estrangement of independent white males."

Some of the Bush-Rove team's advantages were simply gifts. Richards had already served up an easy target soon after Bill Clinton was inaugurated as president in 1993. Lloyd Bentsen was slowing down, and he accepted Clinton's offer to leave the Senate and join his cabinet as treasury secretary. For the life of her, Richards couldn't find a strong Democrat who would accept an appointment to fill Bentsen's seat, and then run in the special election to serve the remainder of his term. Democrats had been so proud of the Class of '82 that they hadn't built a bench, much less a farm system. Democrats who looked at the senatorial race had a strong premonition of what was about to happen to them and shied away, but the public perception was that Richards was just inept. Henry Cisneros and John Sharp—Bullock's successor as comptroller—turned her down. Finally, in exasperation, Richards turned to Bob Krueger, a Shakespearean scholar from Duke University who was by then a two-time loser of U.S. Senate races in Texas. Richards wouldn't have crossed the street for Krueuger during his brief heyday as a conservative Democratic candidate, but she was desperate. After accepting the appointment, Krueger carped about Clinton's presidency—which was the reason he was finally in the Senate. Meanwhile, Rove talked Kay Bailey Hutchison into running against Krueger in the special election. Toward the end of the campaign, Democratic admaker Roy Spence and Garry Mauro talked the usually dignified Krueger into donning shades and a leather jacket in an Arnold Schwarzenegger *Terminator* routine. It was embarrassing—arguably the worst political ad ever aired in Texas. Hutchison won easily, which meant that two of Rove's past clients, Hutchison and Phil Gramm, now held the Texas seats in the U.S. Senate.

Once George W. Bush began his gubernatorial campaign in earnest, Karl Rove and his team proved themselves masters at scrambling Richards' message. Karen Hughes, a former Dallas TV journalist who was now head of a campaign fund called the Associated Republicans of Texas, kept up a steady barrage of attacks against the governor. Rove's team filed an open-records request for over 5,000 employment applications for state jobs filled by Richards and demanded photocopy machines; the governor's counsel trudged off to fight the thing in court. Richards was continually on the defensive. Cryer fended off incoming fire in the governor's press office; a consultant named Chuck McDonald handled the campaign press and lobbed his own shells at Bush and Rove.

"Karl plays as fair as anybody else in politics," McDonald said later. "But he plays for keeps. I always knew where I stood with Karl. I knew he was trying to kill me." On another occasion, McDonald reflected, "He approaches everything as life or death. He does not give off the vibes that you can go and have a beer with him when the game is over."

The ruthlessness and risks he was willing to take for his candidate were captured in a story that *Dallas Morning News* reporter Anne Marie Kilday told her friend Melinda Henneberger of *The New York Times*. Kilday said Rove called her one day during the '94 race and said he was looking at the telephone records of a state official and reputed lesbian, adding that he found it interesting that the official in question made repeated calls to Kilday—"at your residence," he added. Kilday went on: "He said, 'You've just got to be careful about your reputation and what people might think.'"

Rove denied that such a conversation could ever have taken place. "The official's sexuality," he claimed, in any case, "would have had nothing to do with it."

Well, perhaps.

Rove knew he could intimidate reporters on occasion. If Rove thought a reporter had gotten a story wrong or was unfair to Bush, he would call with a loud angry rebuttal. He wasn't always looking for a retraction, but he knew the reporter would write other stories in the future and he wanted to get his message across. (Later, as the presidential campaign got in gear, editors would sometimes hear from the campaign press office about a story Rove considered editorial in tone.)

Meanwhile Bush was as nice to Richards as he could possibly be. He came off in the race as a well-bred young gentleman. Bush had also learned from his dad the peril of ignoring the Christian right; he talked about faith-based social services and the right to life. But neither Rove nor Bush wanted any part of the Hispanic immigrant-bashing espoused by Pat Buchanan and California's Republican governor, Pete Wilson. "Hell, if they'll walk across Big Bend, we want 'em," Bush would say privately about undocumented Mexican workers.

Bush didn't have to do anything to win over one important block of voters. In Richards' first session, legislators had pushed through a bill that would permit Texans to get a license to carry concealed handguns. Richards vetoed it, and law enforcement groups were urgent in their support of her position, but the thing came right back at her. Before one group she answered a question about the bill by saying, "Well, I could support it if they had to wear them around their necks. Everybody would know who's packing. 'Uh-oh, look out for that one—he's got a gun.'" She also ridiculed the idea that women would be safer if armed, saying that as a woman she understood that there was no way any woman would be able to find a gun in her handbag. Gun owners did not find these jibes funny. Bush talked about the sanctity of the Second Amendment and said that he would sign a concealed handgun bill, and he won the votes of angry voters who were spoiling to punish Richards.

Reporters marveled at the efficiency and the detail of George W. Bush's campaign and the skill of the man running it. The 1994 race was when Karl Rove shed his reputation as another hatchet man and became the Boy Genius. He could say he admired Richards as a person and her character was not the issue. But no potentially damaging detail was left unattended. Democrats complained that it was no coincidence when Bill Ratliff—a Rove client and Republican state senator from East Texas, who was known for his principle and integrity—held a press conference in Mount Pleasant and raised the specter of lesbians working for Ann Richards. The story seemed to die among urban sophisticates in Austin, but not among more conservative voters in Longview or Tyler. Push pollsters began to place calls and wonder aloud if people would vote for Richards if they knew she moved in social circles with lesbians, and might be one herself. Reporters were wary of that rumor, and wouldn't touch it. But it was out there.

Though Richards' popularity ratings continued to be high, the mood of her staff revealed the fear that had set in. They stopped sharing information with Bullock and his staff, convinced that he had crossed over and was feeding every tidbit to Bush and Rove. In Richards' debate with Bush, the challenger once more benefited from underestimation. He was polite and respectful. "Thank you, Governor," he said with a nod, when she dismissed a reporter's question about his military service during Vietnam, and then scored the point of the night when he said her expressed reasons for wanting to be governor hadn't changed one bit in four years. There was a day of excitement in her office when Ross Perot, forever trying to pay back those Bushes for some perceived wrong, endorsed her, but the polls didn't move.

That election day in 1994, the Democrats experienced what Rove had felt in the Clements campaign twelve years earlier. They knew. There was a national race, too, the midterm congressional election. Hillary Clinton's health care plan had been a disaster, and Newt Gingrich was coming to power in Congress. After two years the Clinton presidency appeared to be a cinder. That night, with

Bush ahead by more than 300,000 votes, 53 to 47 percent, Richards made her concession speech early. She almost looked relieved.

Stunned commentators attributed her loss to the nationwide repudiation of Bill Clinton, but Richards and her aides knew that wasn't how it happened. They recalled her announcement of her campaign for reelection at a birthday celebration. The country singer Jimmie Dale Gilmore performed, and she had made one of her colorful and fiery speeches, yet the event didn't have a pulse. Neither would her race. The soccer moms who had supported her against the insulting cowboy Clayton Williams went back to being Republicans. She was tired and adrift, and the marathoner Bush just kept coming, always on message. Richards loyalists were left with regrets and the belief that this was a race not just lost but blown. "Karl deserved all the credit he received," his onetime co-worker Bill Cryer said with a sigh. "It was a masterful performance; they did everything right. But let's hear it, too, for the Ann Richards campaign. If it hadn't been for us, George W. Bush wouldn't be president of the United States."

With the election of Bush as governor, the Democrats were finished in Texas, though they could not yet admit it to themselves. With Texas effectively conquered and with a candidate of limitless confidence and possibility, Karl Rove could now turn his sights on the rest of the nation.

PART 2

RISING STAR IN THE LONE STAR STATE

5

Kiss Me First

The roar of approval and adulation that greeted Bush as governor was instantaneous, and it carried him along with hardly a flutter or dip. He had the advantage of being Republican in a state whose electorate had turned that corner, probably for good. The power of the governor's office was extremely limited, had been designed that way and had stayed that way for more than a century. Texans felt they had been abused by the scalawags and carpetbaggers whom the federal government had authorized to serve as governor during Reconstruction, and once that was over and the occupying federal troops were withdrawn, a new constitution had been enacted, in 1876, that would keep any governor from wielding such power again. A legislative attempt to modernize and rewrite the state constitution had collapsed in the mid–1970s, so the Texas government creaked along, changing in small increments. Many ballots contained a list of arcane constitutional amendments, which only a popular vote could authorize, just to keep the government working.

The governor still had power, of course. Education, utilities, insurance, transportation, the environment, the state parks system,

and many other areas were overseen by commissions whose boards
the governor appointed. There was some overlap between the
boards of each governor, so the lurches in policy and direction,
wouldn't be too sudden, but in making those appointments, the
governor charted the path of the bureaucracy. The state senate and
house of representatives met every other year in 140-day sessions,
and that was all the time they had to jam legislation through—
unless the governor called a special session over some emergency,
and most governors were reluctant to do that. Legislators were paid
such a ridiculously low sum, $7,200 a year as previously men-
tioned, that unless the senator or representative had some very
lenient and supportive employers, only rich people could hold the
office, at least for very long. In this way the rule of the establishment was assured.

The speaker of the house was chosen by pledge of the individual
legislators, just as it's done in the U.S. Congress. The lieutenant governor, though, was elected by the people of the state to preside over
the senate, and since there were just thirty-one senators, his power
was less dispersed. The senate defined the lieutenant governor's
power by writing the rules of the body; if the lieutenant governor
was well-liked, or much-feared, then the senators designed the
office in ways that gave their leader great power. The conventional
wisdom was that the lieutenant governor had the real power in
Texas.

The balance of power between governor and lieutenant governor was also measured by personal style and charisma. A John Connally or Ann Richards came to have substantial power as governor;
a Preston Smith or Dolph Briscoe served his term and was soon forgotten. George W. Bush could be arrogant, defensive, and full of

himself, but those facets seldom caught the public eye. He had enormous magnetism and charm; he was a good ol' boy without being smarmy in the way of other notable GOP Southerners like Trent Lott or Haley Barbour. Bush was a relative stranger in Austin, but he was immediately appreciated. He was personable and sophisticated; he and Laura were soon noted and admired for their taste in chefs and restaurants. And in Texas the new governor was buoyed always by a deep reservoir of affection for his dad and mom. Now living in Houston, the elder Bush was immersed in writing his memoirs and building his presidential library in College Station, on the campus of Texas A&M.

The Democrats still had majorities in both houses of the legislature. Some Democrats believed that Bob Bullock had made an open secret of helping Bush's campaign because he was tired of being adored less than his old drinking pal Richards—that Bullock believed this rich kid knew nothing about state government and would be more easily bent to the lieutenant governor's will than Richards had been. There was a story that Barbara Bush had asked Bullock to look out for her son, and he was charmed by her personal request. Whatever the source of their chemistry, Bush and Bullock carried on like soulmates from the start, and Bush was no less adept at swapping yarns about West Texas and small-town life with the house speaker, Pete Laney. The governor got anything he wanted from his first session of the legislature.

Bush also began the seduction of Bob Bullock, which would pay off later. The lieutenant governor had a sinecure at an Austin law firm, but he was not a wealthy man by any means. Bush invited him to fly along and join the family on hunting leases Bullock could never afford—all the while flattering the older man's sense of importance. On one occasion Bush's courtship of Bullock seemed more than a metaphor. The lieutenant governor once complained to Bush, after the governor refused to support him on a particular issue, "If you're going to fuck me, you're going to have to kiss me first." To disarm Bullock, Bush kissed him. Bush would make the mistake of retelling this story during the 2000 presidential campaign to Tucker Carlson, who was writing a profile of him for *Talk* magazine.

A *Texas Monthly* writer asked Karl Rove when it was that he first realized Bush might be presidential timber. "Sometime during the '95 [legislative] session, it dawned on me," he said. "He was a fabulous candidate, but I didn't know how he was going to govern. To see him walk onto a stage with such a complicated cast of characters—Bullock, Laney, Democrats in all the major positions—and difficult personalities and win them over was a revelation."

In many ways Bush's first term as governor of Texas foretold his style and agenda in the White House. There was no way to anticipate the defining moment of his presidency, of course. Governors have no military and foreign policy—no moment in history, as Rove would often put it, that predict that capability as commander in chief. But the Texas agenda proved to be a blueprint for Bush's domestic policy.

There were some housekeeping items and promises to be kept. An early priority was to let Texans have their licenses to carry concealed handguns. Fine—make sure they went to some kind of safety school first. More important to Bush was a tax cut. As comptroller, Bullock had voiced the heresy that Texas was never going to steady its finances unless it instituted a state income tax. Scorched by the political fireworks that went off as a consequence, he retreated from that position, and as lieutenant governor, seemingly in a fit of pique, he maneuvered through the legislature a bill that prohibited the imposition of a state income tax unless voters approved a constitutional amendment. It was vintage Bullock logic—if he couldn't personally chart the state's fiscal future, and institute a change that was needed, then by God nobody was going to. The state collected sales and franchise taxes and increasingly passed the buck to cities, counties, and school districts, so property taxes soared. Tax relief was a middle-class issue. Bush wanted a big tax cut on his record, and with Bullock's and Laney's help he pushed one through. A $7.6 billion surplus on the state's books whistled toward a record deficit as high as $12 billion by 2002. But he delivered on his promises; he was true to his word.

Rove said the angriest he ever saw Bush was that first year. An education bureaucrat came to brief the governor and staff and remarked in passing that 43,000 third-graders in Texas couldn't pass minimal tests for reading skills. Rove described the conversation: "The governor said, 'What happened to the forty-three thousand?' The guy said, 'Well, thirty-nine thousand went on to the fourth grade.' The governor went through the roof." Education reform, universal testing, became his legislative crusade, and the house and senate gave him that as well.

Bush was an oilman, albeit an unsuccessful one; not much was expected of him on the environment. Still, his father had offered the Clean Air Act as one of the intellectual high points of his administration, remarkable coming from a Texas oilman. Apart from what the muck was doing to Texans' lungs, Houston, Dallas-Fort Worth, El Paso, San Antonio, Austin, and smaller urban centers were in continual danger of falling out of compliance with that federal law, and the law had teeth—states that did not ensure compliance could lose billions of dollars in highway funds. The EPA issued a periodic toxic release inventory of contaminants spewed, leaked, or dumped into the environment; in every announcement, Texas ranked first or second to Louisiana. Weeks after he had been elected governor, Bush acknowledged that he had never heard of a toxic release inventory. Bush, his staff, and his advisors blithely ignored the matter of Texas and the Clean Air Act. They would rely on incentives for industry and voluntary compliance.

Bush dismantled Richards' ambitious program of drug and alcohol treatment in the prisons, and Bullock, who had helped her build it, chose not to fight for the program. Such an approach rankled Bush. He didn't need a twelve-step program to overcome *his* drinking problem. He just woke up one morning with a bad hangover and years of guilt, and he quit drinking. Bush said he did it with discipline and faith, and that's what he wanted to see in the prisons. He invited Charles Colson, the Watergate heavy who was born again in federal prison, to introduce his program of prayer in the yards and cellblocks.

The governor had a reputation and air as a moderate. He shunned the Christian Right and disdained the immigrant-bashers in his party. Bush was accepted, even by Democrats who would never vote for him, as a decent country-club Republican, rather like his dad. But he was much more of an ideologue than he let on. People invited to his office to talk about jobs came away stunned by his obsession with privatization. Bush remarked to a South Texas Democratic legislator that he'd love to privatize the University of Texas, though he doubted he would see that in his lifetime. Privatize a public university with 50,000 students on just one of its campuses and an oil-based endowment rivaling those of Harvard and Yale? If Bush could imagine that, why not Social Security?

In taking from the legislature, the governor knew when to give a little in return. Like Arizona and California, Texas had a problem of long-term water supply. The problem was complicated by the state's relative vastness—the state is the size of France or Spain—and by its range of climates, from mosquito-laden swamp in the east to bone-dry desert in the west. The weather was prone to ruinous droughts, and legally, Texas is one of the few states that still subscribed to the right of capture—water, even groundwater, is a private property right. Bob Bullock said the arguments had scarcely varied since he was a legislator in the 1950s, and he wanted a system that would give local communities a way to plan for and protect their water future. He called his proposal Senate Bill 1, a pointed way of stressing its importance to him. Bush helped him find common ground with the rural and industry interests who had gone after Richards with a vengeance when she proposed a similar plan.

From the start Rove was described as a pillar in Bush's "Iron Triangle" of advisors, along with press aide Karen Hughes and chief of staff Joe Allbaugh. But Rove did not go on Bush's state payroll, as he had with his first elected governor, Bill Clements. A few blocks from the Capitol, the consultant spent the days in a windowless Karl Rove + Company office, identifiable by the "Labor for Nixon" bumper sticker on his door. Direct mail specialists are pleased with a 2 percent response rate. Three percent is exceptional and anything over 5 percent is spectacular. When a reporter asked Rove about his

response rates, he pulled out a sheaf of papers. "Here's one where
we got a 24.24 percent response," he began. "Here's one where we
raised about $300,000 on a 24.81 response with an average gift of
$57." He continued reading off the list: "Ten percent. . . . Here's
one with 4 percent, here's one with 18 percent." Rove said the key
to success in direct mail is having "the right list, with the right message at the right time. It has to grab attention and it has to be based
in fact and need."

The tall, articulate, ever-forceful Hughes was Bush's communications director and most visible policy adviser. Allbaugh (now
director of the Federal Emergency Management Administration)
was a bluff, loud man who had worked for an Oklahoma governor
and who presented a startling figure to Austin slackers. He had a
brush cut—not a crewcut, he stressed—that was greased and stood
straight up; a "flat top" was the Texas term for the look when it was
current about half a century earlier. He came on like a high school
football coach from that era.

The ideologies of Bush and Rove were most aligned in the team's
approach to social services. Bush and Rove had come through their
youth in the war-protesting, drug-taking sixties with vastly different
backgrounds and personal experiences, but they were joined at the
hip in one conviction: That was a time in the nation's life deserving
of revulsion, not nostalgia.

Their ideological creed was a 1993 book by Myron Magnet
called *The Dream and the Nightmare: the Sixties' Legacy to the
Underclass.* Magnet, a *Fortune* magazine writer and a fellow at the
Manhattan Institute for Policy Research, contended that lazy minds
bred by the sixties (such as that of Bill Clinton) had passed on their
notions of free love and self-fulfillment to the poor, ruining their
chances of pulling themselves out of poverty by their own boot-

straps. Magnet wrote that the counterculture "withdrew respect from the behavior and attitudes that have traditionally boosted people up the economic ladder—deferral of gratification, sobriety, thrift, and so on—through the whole catalogue of antique-sounding bourgeois virtues." In his office Rove had a shelf full of copies of Magnet's book, and he handed them out like Bibles.

In their zeal for privatization and welfare reform, Bush and his team wanted to bury whatever remained of Lyndon Johnson's Great Society and remind the nation of its heritage of faith-based social services. That was a delicate pitch to sell, even in Texas. There was the constitutional requirement of separation of church and state, for starters. Also, Texas had a sorry past of religious schools for poor and unwanted kids that had been licensed by the state and run, to politicians' embarrassment, like concentration camps. (The Lester Roloff homes that John Hill had shut down as attorney general were only the most egregious example.) The Bush team's most tireless and vocal critic was an organization called the Texas Freedom Network. It raised a steady drumbeat of fear and antagonism toward the Religious Right. The group's founder and spokesperson was Cecile Richards, the ex-governor's daughter.

There was another issue the Bush team had to be careful with, one that would reappear during his run for the White House. Bush got less than 9 percent of the black vote in his race against Richards, and the rejection puzzled and bothered him—he described that as the one major disappointment of his campaign. Myron Magnet's disdain for hippies and draft-dodgers was easy for him to defend intellectually—in his view they were losers in a sorry time that was long past, and most had continued to demonstrate their shiftless-ness and mediocrity. Outside of a diminishing slice of popular cul-ture, such people had few defenders; all the relevance they had now was negative. But the argument that their glamorization had soaked into and contaminated the values of the underclass was a riskier jump to make—especially if Bush and Rove wanted to carry that leap into politics and social policy. At best, Magnet's value judgments implied a condescension toward people who were poor. An overwhelming majority of Texans living in poverty were black and Hispanic. The perception of being haughty white lords over poor people of color was a bogey that Republicans were trying hard to shake.

The wordsmith who could sell these concepts to the general public turned out to be right under the Republicans' noses. On the University of Texas journalism faculty was a tall, ungainly, immensely confident man named Marvin Olasky. He had grown up Jewish in New York, a doctrinaire leftist, but then underwent a crisis of spirit and came out of it born again, a philosopher of the Christian right. Olasky wrote columns for editorial pages of Texas newspapers, and they had caught the eye of the governor and his strategists. Soon Olasky was a regular in the governor's office, briefing aides on the fundamentalist philosophy and how it could be applied. He gave them the feel-good term and concept they were looking for: compassionate conservatism.

6

Two Birds with One Stone

Not every conservative Christian was as enthusiastic and effusive about George W. Bush as was Marvin Olasky, the avatar of compassionate conservatism. In fact, there was one high-profile Christian in the Texas Republican Party leadership whom Rove would gladly have banished to a Trappist monastery, where a code of silence is strictly enforced.

Karl Rove's fight with Tom Pauken began in 1994. It involved the one faction in the party Rove had underestimated: the evangelical Christians who had come into the Republican fold with Pat Robertson's 1988 presidential campaign. Nowhere had their strength been more evident than at the 1994 Republican state convention in Fort Worth. Christian Right delegates filled the convention center two blocks from the hotel where John Kennedy spent the night of November 21, 1963. Prayer breakfasts drew bigger crowds than hospitality suites. The virtuous William Bennett came in first in the presidential straw vote. Texas Senator Phil Gramm won only 8 percent of the pool because he was soft on defense of the unborn. Every winning candidate (and most losing candidates) for party office praised God and excoriated abortion. And U.S. Senator Kay Bailey Hutchison was booed when she stood up to address the convention. Not because of anything she said in her speech, but because she openly supported women's reproductive rights.

Rove could count.

He knew he had lost control of the party. But with his new candidate, George W. Bush, then starting a race for the governorship against an incumbent with approval ratings in the 60s and 70s, Rove had to control the party chairmanship. The new evangelical majority had already thrown out Fred Meyer, George H. W. Bush's handpicked chairman, and were backing Tom Pauken, a Dallas lawyer who had run the ACTION volunteers program for Ronald Reagan. Pauken was a stout, pugilistic conservative who had run two bruising if losing campaigns against Jim Mattox, a liberal Democratic congressman from Dallas. He was backed by an uncompromising faction Rove couldn't control. So Rove recruited his own candidate: Dallas-area Congressman Joe Barton, who spent three days campaigning under the rubric "Pro-Life Joe." Barton—one of Rove's first clients when he ran for the U.S. House race in 1984—showed up with an impressive list of supporters: Senators Gramm and Hutchison, both elected to office under the guidance of Karl Rove; most of the Republican delegation in the U.S. House; and the party's new marquee star, the son of the President of the United States, George W. Bush.

The Christian delegates weren't impressed.

The fight for the state chair was a rare miscalculation for Rove. Even if he was fighting within the confines of the party, the pragmatist known for picking winning candidates had picked a fight he couldn't win. It was over before the first "Grand Old Prayer Session" drew 3,500 delegates on the opening day of the convention.

But Rove and Barton wouldn't let it go. The vote was set for Saturday. By early Friday evening the beleaguered Congressman Barton was barking at his operatives: "I'm tired of hearing what I can't do. I want to see their cards. I want *them* to prove *they* can do it." Rove continued to beat the dead horse on which he had bet $100,000 in campaign cash and the political future of George W. Bush.

When Barton finally saw the Christian delegates' cards, he folded. Tom Pauken held 3,076 commitments to Joe Barton's 2,162. Instead of a floor fight on the final day of the convention, delegates embraced a platform that supported constitutional rights for the unborn, the repeal of the Clean Air Act and the Endangered Species Act, the end of the state's authority to compel children to attend school, a repeal of the minimum wage, and a return to the gold standard. Eight years later, only the quaint monetary policy seems extreme in the context of a Congress led by Majority Leader Tom DeLay. Yet Bush immediately distanced himself from his party's platform.

Rove and Bush came to an important strategic conclusion in Fort Worth. To govern on behalf of the corporate right, they would have to appease the Christian right. Both Rove and Bush were pragmatic economic conservatives. Rove would say he had no great abiding faith, and only when Bush began his campaign for the presidency would he begin to speak more openly about his religious beliefs. Neither of the men were Pat Robertson Republicans. But the 1994 convention taught them a valuable lesson. The party's economic conservatives and social conservatives had to be kept in harness.

What was learned in Fort Worth was evident in Bush's accommodation of the Christian conservatives' agenda and his zealous

pursuit of the business community's agenda after he became governor. It was also evident when Rove retained the services of Ralph
Reed, who had served as executive director of the Christian Coalition, as Bush prepared to enter the Republican presidential primaries.

They also concluded that Tom Pauken had to go.

Yet Pauken had fallen in line (more or less), coming to the same
conclusion reached by Rove and Bush. The marriage of the Christian conservatives and the economic conservatives had to be made to
work if the party was to work. This marriage, after all, defines the
modern Republican Party. Pauken sparred with Rove but was well
behaved during Bush's first legislative session in 1995. As Bush's
second biennial session got underway in 1997, though, Pauken
appeared to be testing the limits of his uneasy domestic relationship
with Bush and Rove. And he was doing so at a time when Bush was
preparing to use his success in managing the Texas Legislature to
quietly begin his campaign for the presidency.

In January of that year, Pauken entered the race to succeed Mississippi lobbyist Haley Barbour as chairman of the national Republican Party. Rove would have been happy to see Pauken leave Texas,
but not if he were moving into the national headquarters of the
Republican Party. So the campaign against Pauken began. Rove's
old client, Bill Clements, began calling around the country inform-
ing high-level Republicans that Pauken was damaged goods.

Pauken claimed that Clements, by that time almost eighty years
old and retired from politics, had offered him a job if he would
withdraw from the election for the Republican national party chairmanship. He also accused the senior George Bush of pressing
Clements to nudge him out of the race for party chair. According to

Pauken, the former president feared that if Pauken were Republican National Committee chairman, he would get in the way of George W.'s 2000 presidential race.

"Nuts," Clements said. "It's just nuts."

"Baloney," he said. "All of that is just absolute baloney." Clements said he had met with Pauken for two hours, but there had been no job offer. And certainly no discussion of any presidential campaign. Pauken held his ground, saying he would not "be bought."

Colorado developer Jim Nicholson won the national eight-candidate race and Pauken kept his job as chairman of the Republican Party in Texas. But the feud continued. Rove saw to it that many big Republican funders did not contribute to the party. Pauken saw to it that Karl Rove + Company lost the Republican Party's direct mail contract. If this lacked the intensity and drama of the feud between Lyndon Johnson and Texas Senator Ralph Yarborough, it nevertheless made it more difficult for Rove to prepare for a presidential campaign.

Pauken also created a problem in the Legislature. The Texas Legislature meets every two years for 140 days, and some careful observers of the process have made the case that meeting for two days every 140 years might be preferable. The same constitutional framers who feared placing too much power in the hands of the governor also feared placing too much power in the hand of the Legislature. So sessions are biennial and salaries are laughable. The business lobby perennially includes at least 1,500 registered members, who spend approximately $250 million each session in their efforts to influence the votes of 181 legislators. Thus every two years the Texas Legislature becomes a bottleneck through which only the bills of the most powerful, most plaintive, most persistent, or most devious interests can pass.

A governor can draw up an agenda and get in line with competing interests. Or he can use his political skills and expend his political capital to get his own legislative package enacted. Bush's first session, in 1995, won rave reviews from the critics. He charmed legislators by connecting with them individually. And he delivered on his campaign promises of tort reform, more prisons, a more punitive juvenile justice system, and some education reform. "Like a knife through butter," was how lobbyist Bill Miller described Bush's run through the Legislature in 1995.

After he lost his race for the national committee chair, Tom Pauken returned to Texas and settled into the 1997 legislative process like a tropical depression. The big reform proposal Bush was delicately moving through the Legislature would have replaced the state's creaky corporate franchise tax with a tax on partnerships. (The franchise tax functioned like an income tax on corporations, but limited partnerships were exempt, so many businesses escaped taxation.) Property taxes would have been reduced. And lost revenue would be replaced by taxes on goods and services. It is a cultural imperative that Republicans don't raise taxes, so the governor's staff and the governor promised that whatever they passed would be "revenue-neutral." No new money would be raised.

To Pauken, increasing any tax or taxing something heretofore untaxed was a tax increase—even if another tax was lowered. "It's not a tax cut, it's a tax hike," Pauken told reporters at a Capitol press conference. He described Bush's ambitious proposal as a scheme to "give us something in one hand and then take it back in another." At times it was impossible to tell whether the hit sheets attacking the Republican governor's tax plan were faxed from the offices of Democratic Party Chair Bill White or Republican Party Chair Tom Pauken.

Pauken urged Republican legislators to vote against the bill. He even bought newspaper ads attacking "Governor Bush's Tax Increase." And he succeeded in persuading Republicans to vote against their governor's tax measure, which only passed in the House because Democrats supported it. The proposal finally died in the Republican-controlled Senate. Bush would have to wait two more years for a campaign sound bite describing him as "the governor who cut property taxes for all Texans."

Pauken didn't feel as if he had to wait until the current session ended. The tax bill was dead, but Pauken still tried to hang it around Bush's neck. "It's like something you would expect from a liberal Democrat," he told *Washington Post* reporter Sue Anne Pressley in May 1997.

Here was a *Post* reporter in Austin working a softball page-one story about George W. Bush. Everything was falling into place for Rove. A former LBJ aide was talking Texan, observing that Bush didn't seem to be doubled over with ambition: "The best politics is an easygoing politics. Some of these fellas overdo it when they try to run for something." A Republican legislator was cultivating the log cabin myth. "When George moved back to Midland, he bummed an office, he bummed golf clubs, bummed shoes." Even the Democratic Party's press flack was singing Bush's praises: "Some people thought he was not the brightest porch light on the block, and they were wrong about that." The lone critical voice in a national daily story that framed Bush as a leading contender for the presidency just happened to be the chairman of the Republican Party of Texas.

Rove and his surrogates couldn't get their hooks into Pauken. But later in 1997, the Texas party chairman made a move that would put him directly in Karl Rove's gunsights. He announced he would run for the Republication nomination for attorney general. It was the opportunity Rove had been waiting for. He didn't have a mechanism to move Pauken out of the party chairmanship. But he did know how to win elections.

The 1998 attorney general's election was one of the most peculiar races in a state known for its peculiar politics. And it almost requires a playbill to follow it from start to finish. Rove wanted to seize the moment and send Tom Pauken back to his Dallas law practice. But he also wanted to defeat the Democratic incumbent, Dan Morales, an attractive, unpredictable Hispanic who was often mentioned as a candidate for governor.

Morales was almost a perfect Democratic candidate. A Mexican-American from a middle-class family in San Antonio, Morales had attended preppy Trinity University in San Antonio and Harvard Law School. Out of Harvard, he worked as a prosecutor, a lawyer in a corporate law firm, and a state representative. He was a boyish-looking thirty-four when he was elected attorney general. This dapper Hispanic—trim, telegenic, and slightly dweeby—had more crossover appeal than Antonio Banderas. He turned on Mexican-American voters while turning out suburban women—and the middle-class white men who often eluded the Democrats. If his Spanish wasn't as good as that of George W. Bush, he had the surname to sell to Hispanic voters. And Morales was the only Democrat whose name would appear near the top of the ballot. His unanticipated, spectacular, vertical collapse—largely of his own doing—had all the intrigue and melodrama of a Mexican telenovela.

In the run-up to the 1998 election, Morales was the candidate who most worried George Bush. "The entire focus was on Morales. Bush did not want Dan Morales. He did not want Morales to win," said a Republican campaign consultant to the 1998 election. Morales was the last star in the Democratic Party's fading constellation, the only Democratic incumbent on the statewide ballot. If he could be eliminated—and the Democrats running for open seats defeated—the party that eight years earlier had a lock on every statewide office would hold none. And every statewide office is a power base, providing patronage, employment for campaign operatives, publicity platforms, and a farm team to develop new talent.

Eliminating Morales was a critical step in Rove's project of dismantling the party from the top down. If he could do it in 1998, a Republican sweep from the top of the ballot down would be easier to achieve in 2002. Morales had also talked about running for governor. At the top or close to the top of the ballot, a star with Morales' crossover appeal would discourage some voters from voting the straight Republican ticket that was becoming more common in Texas.

Rove also had a personal reason for targeting Dan Morales. A year into Bush's first term, the Democratic attorney general had filed suit against the nation's big tobacco companies, to recover some of the money the state had incurred in treating tobacco-related illness. To prepare for the lawsuit, the lawyers Morales hired to represent the state decided to question Rove. Pitting a strong candidate against Morales also allowed Rove to settle the score with the attorney general who had dragged him into a lawyer's office, put him under oath, and subjected him to a deposition by Democratic trial lawyers hired to represent the state in a lawsuit against the tobacco industry.

To kill two birds—Pauken and Morales—with one stone, Rove recruited to the Republican side of the race John Cornyn, a San Antonio lawyer who had once earned a living defending insurance companies, and who remained a faithful friend of the industry in the votes he cast as a justice on the Texas Supreme Court. Trim, tall, courtly, and blessed with prematurely white hair, Cornyn had more box-office appeal than the shorter, stocky Pauken. But because the Supreme Court is invisible to most voters—the Court of Criminal Appeals is the rocket-docket forum to executions in Texas—Cornyn didn't have the high profile Pauken did. So Rove's handpicked candidate entered the race trailing Tom Pauken.

As the state's Republican Party chairman, Tom Pauken was an irritant for George Bush. As the state's independent attorney general he would be a real threat. And it appeared that the underfunded Pauken, with broad-based support from hardcore Reagan Republicans and evangelical Christians, would defeat Rove's handpicked candidate, until an odd thing happened. Barry Williamson, a Republican who was leaving the Texas Railroad Commission to run for comptroller, changed his mind and joined the attorney general's race. Williamson had won his first election to statewide office four years earlier, when Rove was advising his campaign. His entry in the race, with $1 million to spend, meant that two candidates, both flush with cash and both linked to Karl Rove, were now running against Tom Pauken.

"Rove was not supposed to get involved in Republican primaries," said a source close to the Cornyn campaign. Rove was so formidable that Republican candidates didn't want him in the primaries. "But Pauken was in the race," the campaign source said. "And Bush hated Pauken. So the whole idea was that in a three-man race, Rove could see that Cornyn was elected." Williamson became the political equivalent of a *banderillero*, the bullring cape man who works on foot, sticking small barbs into the bull's neck—to provoke it and make it charge, while lowering its head to make it easier for the matador to complete the kill.

While Williamson was lowering Pauken's head, Rove was raising the profile of the real candidate in the race. "Karl was worried about Cornyn's name," the Cornyn campaign source said. "He said it was a bad name for politics. Nobody could pronounce it. And John didn't have an issue to run on. So Karl decided he should file the tobacco suit."

Here was another stone to hit his two birds. The tobacco suit that Rove had Cornyn file, according to this campaign source, was a challenge to the contingency fees that had been earned by five attorneys the state had hired to sue the tobacco industry. That original suit had been filed in 1996 by Dan Morales.

The suit had been a difficult issue for Bush. As governor, he had to support going to court to recover billions the state had spent on health care for indigent patients with tobacco-related illnesses. Yet he opposed industry-wide lawsuits like the cases several states already filed against the tobacco industry. Bush had run for office promising tort reform. "Putting an end to junk lawsuits that clog our courts," was a Rove one-liner Bush repeated like a mantra while campaigning. He was successfully pushing a package of tort reforms through the Legislature. And the tobacco companies were major Republican Party donors and underwriters of the party's national conventions. Bush also knew there was neither sufficient staff nor money for the attorney general to undertake the lawsuit. As Mississippi had done, Texas had to retain lawyers on contingency fee. This arrangement would cost the state nothing up front, but if the state prevailed, the fees would enrich the plaintiffs' lawyers hired by the state. And most (if not all) plaintiffs' lawyers, or trial lawyers, are Democrats. Derided by the senior George Bush as "trial lawyers in tassel loafers," they were the very Democratic funders George W. Bush believed had defeated his father.

The governor was in a box.

So was Rove.

As the governor's campaign strategist, Rove was the architect of the campaign Bush ran against the state's trial lawyers. He helped devise the tort reform program Bush was pushing through the Legislature. And he had a personal conflict. From 1991 to 1996, Rove worked for Philip Morris, the tobacco company with the largest market share in Texas and the nation, earning $3,000 a month. And the way monetary damages are awarded in multiple-defendant lawsuits, Rove's client would take the biggest hit if the state collected on tobacco-related health costs.

The tobacco companies had made Rove's difficult position ever more difficult. In an effort to discourage Morales from suing them, Philip Morris, R. J. Reynolds, Lorillard, and Brown & Williamson hired a political consultant to conduct a push poll targeting Morales. Rove wasn't a tobacco company executive, employee, or even a lobbyist. So he would not be named a party to a tobacco suit. But his professional relationship with Philip Morris made him a potential witness—putting him in the one position political operatives and presidents try very hard to avoid: under oath. The tobacco companies' push poll made that even more likely. Push polls test public support of candidates while measuring the effect of negative information provided by the pollster. They are sometimes used to disseminate negative information—which doesn't have to be true because it is presented as a hypothetical—to "drive up the negatives" on a candidate. In the Morales poll, a straightforward question that asked about support for Morales was followed by a question that asked if it were known that Morales supported the causes of Louis Farrakhan and the Nation of Islam. If the pollster conducts enough telephone interviews or mails out enough polls, he begins a public discussion about Morales' work with Farrakhan, which never occurred. Tobacco's push poll on Morales did in fact link him to Farrakhan, as well as to several other issues which were anathema in Texas: affirmative action, out-of-control youth gangs, and gun control. (Affirmative action was the unkindest cut of them all, as Morales had angered his own party by supporting and expanding a federal appeals court ruling against race-based admissions to the University of Texas Law School.)

Rove had been consulted in the design of the poll and several weeks later was summoned to the office of Philip Morris' Austin lobbyist, Jack Dillard, when the lobby group met to discuss the results of the poll.

A year after Morales filed suit against the tobacco companies—with the reluctant public blessing of Governor Bush—Rove was sitting in the office of a Democratic plaintiffs' lawyer. Under oath, Rove was answering questions about his work as a Philip Morris consultant—and whatever other questions the lawyer from the state's tobacco trial team wanted answered. After Rove was questioned, Morales released transcripts of the deposition to reporters.

This was not a common practice, although depositions are public record.

News accounts of the four-hour deposition were an embarrassment to Rove. Under oath he insisted that in order to avoid a conflict of interest, he never spoke with the governor about tobacco issues. Yet he was forced to admit that he delivered the results of the push poll to Bush executive assistant Joe Allbaugh. After admitting he served as a courier for the tobacco lobby, Rove backtracked. Yes, he had delivered the poll, he said, but only because he knew Allbaugh would never let Bush see it: "If Allbaugh had said let's go show it to the governor, I don't think we ought to. This is a matter between Philip Morris and Morales. I think we ought to ditch the poll."

It required a grueling thirty minutes to get Rove to the position of admitting he had done what he had done:

Q. Isn't it fair to say that you had contact with the office of the Governor on an issue related to tobacco when you said you weren't going to do that?
A. Fine. Yeah.
Q. That is correct, isn't it. Your answer is yes?
A. No.

The lawyers continued until Rove angrily agreed, or almost agreed, that he had been in contact with Bush's office on a tobacco-related issue.

It's rare that a political consultant's core beliefs are tested under oath, but pressed by the Mississippi trial lawyer, Rove even got in a riff on tort reform. He said he had crafted Bush's message about the excessive influence of trial lawyers. He referred to the "utility of frivolous and junk suits as a political issue." And when pressed to explain frivolous lawsuits, Rove responded with the anecdotal bite tort reformers routinely rely on to support their position:

> The woman from North Texas who buys her son a car or a grandson a car to drive back and forth to community college in Oklahoma and then gets sued when he has an accident. Or the guy in Lubbock who lends a ladder to his neighbor and then proceeds to get sued by his neighbor when his neighbor falls off the ladder for not having instructed him properly that the ladder is dangerous.

Suddenly, in the context of a contentious deposition, without missing a lick, the deponent shifted into the campaign mode:

> And my opinion is that there are too many lawsuits and too many frivolous claims by people against other people, that the legal system is jerry-rigged. And it's rigged in a certain way.

Gesturing in the direction of the portly lawyer interrogating him, Rove said there are health risks with certain products like saccharine, but the tradeoff is the health risks related to obesity.

In the end the state's lawyers got little they could have used in court. And Rove never took the witness stand. But the industry settled with the state for $17 billion, and $3 billion in legal fees that would be paid separately by the tobacco companies. The five trial lawyers were going to collect paychecks that would put them in a tax bracket with Halliburton's Dick Cheney, Enron's Ken Lay, or GM's Jack Welch. It was more than Rove could stomach. Billions in discretionary income in the hands of five men with a history of underwriting Democratic candidates could undo all the party-building Rove had accomplished since arriving in Texas twenty years earlier. After all, Texas is the Wild West of Campaign Finance: Any individual can give any amount of money to any candidate, as long as it is declared. The tobacco fees might mean that Democratic candidates for statewide office would have access to the kind of financial backing that had heretofore been available only to Republicans.

It was at this point that Rove pushed John Cornyn into the Beaux Arts federal courthouse that sits astride the state line in Texarkana, where the complex tobacco suit had just been settled. Cornyn—who had resigned from the Supreme Court to run for an office that would make him the lawyer for the state of Texas—stood in the courtroom and announced that he was "a private citizen" intervening in a multibillion-dollar lawsuit that all the involved parties had agreed was over. And Judge David Folsom—who over two years had presided over hundreds of hearings, ruled on the admissibility of hundreds of thousands of documents, and resolved countless disputes between tobacco company lawyers and lawyers hired by the state—suddenly must have regretted leaving a lucrative law practice to preside over a courtroom being turned into a stage for second-rate political melodrama. (And it would only get worse. Bush filed his own motion to intervene, sending staff attorneys to Texarkana to take on the attorney general and the trial lawyers. It's hard to imagine Bush would take such an action without consulting Rove. It's also a safe assumption that Rove was consulted when Bush wisely withdrew his motion after several months.)

If jumping into a settled case was an egregious abuse of the federal court system, it was also smart politics. The candidate with the name that no one could pronounce had found his issue. Though the legal fees were set by an arbitration panel acceptable to all parties, did not come out of the state's $17 billion settlement, and would revert to the tobacco companies if overturned, Cornyn could claim he was defending Texans against greedy trial lawyers.

In a bolt from the blue, Dan Morales announced in December 1997 that he was not running for reelection, and he was subsequently investigated by the feds for trying to secure a half billion dollar legal fee for an attorney he had secretly brought into the tobacco case. In the Republican race, Cornyn forced Pauken into a runoff and Williamson out of elective office and into the daily schmooze of the corporate lobby. Then, with $1.5 million provided by a tort-reform PAC and hundreds of thousands of dollars from the tobacco companies, Cornyn sent the underfunded Tom Pauken back home to Dallas.

Two years later in his law office, Pauken reflected on his defeat. "When I became party chair," he said, "Karl discouraged people from giving to the party. The whole time I was chair, we didn't get any Enron money, because Karl was close to those people and dissuaded them. It was difficult." So Pauken knew what to expect when he entered the attorney general's race. He would get little money from the party's big corporate donors. And he would campaign against a candidate selected and managed by Karl Rove. "Cornyn was Karl's candidate in the AG race," Pauken said. What Pauken didn't anticipate was a third candidate brought to serve as a spoiler. In the end he was outspent and outsmarted by Bush's Boy Genius. Pauken believes that Rove called the shots at Williamson's campaign, or at least that the political consultant running Williamson's campaign was a little too tight with Karl Rove.

"Rove was close to the Williamson campaign, to that heavy-set campaign manager from the Northeast," Pauken said. "Heavy-set" is a bit of an understatement. David Carney, brought in from New Hampshire to run Williamson's campaign, stands six-four and weighs 325 pounds. Like Rove, he was a disciple of the late Lee Atwater. His negative ads, directed at both Cornyn and Pauken, seemed to hurt Pauken most. With no money to buy TV, Pauken couldn't respond.

"I'm not mad at him," Pauken said of Rove. "I beat him. He beat me. That's life: I'm in political exile, and Karl's running the country."

Now Rove had the opportunity to dispose of the last member of the Democrats' celebrated class of '82. Running in Dan Morales' place was former Democratic Attorney General Jim Mattox, first elected to statewide office with Ann Richards, Jim Hightower, Garry Mauro, and Mark White. Rove directed John Cornyn's disciplined, well-financed, campaign against Mattox—the last of the traditional "lib-lab" Democrats—those who represented the liberal-labor wing of Texas' Democratic Party. Mattox was once known as the junkyard dog of Texas politics because of his aggressive campaign tactics. In 1998, he met his match. With Karl Rove calling the shots, John Cornyn won the race. Four years later, he would be elected to the United States Senate, and the fight Karl Rove started over the $3 billion the lawyers earned representing the state would still be tied up in a district court in Houston.

Set in low relief in the transcript of Rove's deposition in the initial suit—the one that may have portended the end of the career of Dan Morales—is a professional résumé so extraordinary that it must be considered more newsworthy than the embarrassing accounts of Rove's four hours under oath.

In the course of questioning Rove about his background, Mississippi trial lawyer Charles Mikhail put down on paper a professional profile of the man who at the time remained largely behind the scenes. There were interesting bits of news, such as Rove's admission for the first time that he had helped on George W. Bush's 1978 congressional race—which Bush had to deny at the time because Rove was perceived to be too liberal in the West Texas district where Bush was running. And Rove's mention of filing suit against former U.S. Attorney General Richard Thornburgh—after he failed to pay a bill he incurred when Karl Rove + Company ran his failed senatorial race in Pennsylvania in 1991. But what is truly stunning is the account of Rove's work in Texas since he answered the call of the elder George Bush in 1977.

In 1981, with the financial support of one of the state's Republican aristocrats, polo playing South Texas rancher Tobin Williams, Rove founded the direct mail consulting firm, Karl Rove + Company. The list of Republican clients—and one Democrat (Phil Gramm in 1982)—defines the remaking of the political landscape in Texas:

Q. Mr. Rove, in the state of Texas other than Senator Hutchison and Governor Bush, what other clients have you had in political campaigns?

A. I'm not going to be able to remember them all, but Governor Clements in '86. Railroad Commissioner Kent Hance in '88. Treasurer [Kay Bailey] Hutchison's '90 race. State Senate campaigns at various times of Teel Bivins. Troy Fraser, Robert Duncan, Florence Shapiro, David Sibley, Bill Ratliff, Steve Ogden. I'm leaving somebody out in the Senate. State House, a number of State House races. Todd Staples, Troy Fraser when he was in the House. Congressman Lamar Smith. Congressman Joe Barton.

Q. Members of the Supreme Court?

A. Every Republican member of the Supreme Court. Railroad Commissioner Barry Williamson. Railroad Commissioner Carole Rylander.

Rove was working from memory and forgot Hance's 1990 primary race for governor. Six months after the deposition, the only Democratic justice on the nine-member Supreme Court would retire to be replaced by a Rove client. And John Cornyn might have been counted twice; he was leaving the Supreme Court to run for attorney general.

News is what's happening at the moment. But an accurate subhead to the *Austin American-Statesman* headline, "State Lawyers Grill Bush Aide About Tobacco Role," would have pointed to a story of far more durable news value. It might have read: "Rove Admits to Making Texas a Republican State."

"What's your batting average?" the lawyer asked Rove.

Rove responded as if he'd been asked to state his name.

"Pretty high."

7

God Bless Texas

As the 1996 presidential race approached, George W. Bush politely and firmly voiced his support for Texas' distinguished U.S. senator, Phil Gramm. A former Texas A&M economics professor, Gramm had started his political career with an unsuccessful conservative Democratic challenge to Lloyd Bentsen in 1982. Then, with Karl Rove's help, he had won a central Texas congressional seat as a Democrat. Gramm announced next that he was switching parties and was going to resign his seat, so that people could decide if they still wanted him. Gramm had made his switch to the Republicans come off like an act of courage. When John Tower decided not to seek reelection to his U.S. Senate seat in 1984, Gramm moved in, destroying a liberal Austin legislator named Lloyd Doggett in one of the meanest campaigns ever directed by Rove. The quip, "Even his friends don't like him," dogged Gramm's angry and rather solitary march through Washington's halls of power.

Following the rout of the Democrats in the 1994 midterm elections, Gramm concluded that he was just the man to put an end to the presidency of Bill Clinton. In a speech that became the earmark of his campaign, Gramm bawled that he had "the best friend a politician can have—money," a line that Rove surely did not supply his former client.

The Gramm presidential race was a disaster: Republicans could not be persuaded to see their future in a man with the visage and mien of a snapping turtle. Whom could they turn to? Steve Forbes? Pat Buchanan? Bob Dole, the old reliable, finally got his turn, and persuaded Jack Kemp to join him on the ticket. Conservative Republicans watched the election unfold in fury and disbelief as Clinton cruised to an effortless reelection.

Amid the grumbling, the Texas governor's presidential campaign edged toward its dawn. "There's no magic moment," Karl Rove would say of how people were responding to George W. Bush, "but sometime during the '96 campaign, you know, people were saying, 'You've done such a marvelous job here. Why don't you—I wish you were the candidate. I wish you were the vice presidential running mate.' . . . It was other people coming to him and saying, 'Think about this.' And his first reaction was dismissive, and then shortly after the '96 elections there's the story about Karen [Hughes] coming in with a poll saying he was the front-runner. And somewhere in that period of time, somewhere in those passage of months after '96 he began to seriously think about it."

Rove went on: "There were three separate wars to be fought, and one of them was the preliminary for the nomination—to win the pre-primary primary. Then there was the primary process and then the general election. And, yes, there were battle plans for each one of them, and, yes, we began thinking about them. A lot of people began thinking about them relatively early, that is to say sometime in '96. Late '96, early '97 there were some discussions, but then serious work in '97 and early '98."

The first challenge, which Phil Gramm never rose beyond, was money. "There would be the primary of money," Rove said. "You know, could you raise the amount of money necessary. . . . The general conventional wisdom was $25 million by the end of the year prior to the primary season." Rove stroked the governor's ego, telling him he already knew how to run for the presidency—the 1994 campaign in Texas had been a sneak preview. "That really was the model for the 2000 campaign," Rove said. "It was, 'Okay, if I'm going to run, I've got to have a vision.' In fact that was his big issue. . . . 'Do I feel I've got something worthy to take to the country? And if I do, I'll run. If I don't, I won't.'"

The questions of capability did not just concern the candidate, of course. The Republicans had just suffered two straight disasters in presidential elections, and Karl Rove was as likely as anyone to lead them out of the wilderness. "No, I haven't run a national campaign, but who has?" he growled. "Jim Baker?" Rove was impudently biting the hand that once generously fed him, perhaps not realizing that the campaign would need to make use of Baker before it was all over. But Rove knew from 1994 that the most successful call to political action was one that looked to the future and claimed it. George W. Bush would not be elected if his campaign was perceived as a re-run of his dad's presidency, with the same aging cast of characters. "Do you populate the campaign with people from 1908?" he asked rhetorically. "No!"

Rove wanted to cultivate the impression of a spontaneous groundswell of people eager to support Bush. From Austin the call went out to issues advisers, GOP members of congress, grassroots organizers. In the meantime, the governor would win reelection in a display of his enormous popularity in Texas. Which was genuine, as Democrats knew all too well.

Someone had asked Ann Richards what she would have done differently if she had known she was going to have just one term. "Oh, I would have raised a little more hell," she replied. After her loss she made a Super Bowl commercial debating the merits of potato chips with her partner in sudden retirement, former New York governor Mario Cuomo. She embarked on a new life as a consultant and corporate board member, on the go between New York, Washington, and Mexico City. She achieved even greater fame as a guest pundit on the political talk shows, and she was making money for the first time in her life. When she was back in Austin she went to movies with her old friend and steady date, the writer Bud Shrake. She liked not having to be chaperoned by a trooper from the Department of Public Safety. And she knew the numbers in Texas. She wasn't about to seek a rematch with George W. Bush. As a candidate she was through.

Who could run against Bush, then? The smooth and urbane former mayor of San Antonio, Henry Cisneros, the Hamlet of Texas Democratic politics, was in Clinton's cabinet as the Secretary of Housing and Urban Development. But during a routine background check, Cisneros had lied to the FBI about money he had paid to his former mistress, and ultimately would plead guilty to a misdemeanor count of lying to a federal official. Bob Bullock had signaled that he wouldn't be running for any office next time around. The business-oriented comptroller, John Sharp, was ballyhooed as the Democrats' great white hope, but he wanted no part of a dust-up with Bush.

Sharp had been a state senator and claimed to love the legislative process; he wanted to succeed Bullock as lieutenant governor. Sharp was among the Democrats who believed the best politics was to concede the top spot on the ballot and make the presidential contender run against nobody. It would keep straight-ticket Republican voters at home and give candidates for other offices, like Sharp, a better chance. The argument was a measure of just how dispirited and marginalized the Democrats had become in Texas.

Sharp and land commissioner Garry Mauro had been student leaders together at Texas A&M, and in the years since they had been allies and friends and increasingly bitter rivals. Finally seeing his chance for the governorship, Mauro decided he would run.

Mauro worked hard to tidy up his image. During his travails in the eighties, reporters would smirk and speculate on who had done the perm of his signature curly locks, until Mauro and his wife had a son with the identical curly hair. Someone convinced Mauro it was time to change his hairstyle, and that may have been a mistake. Before, he at least had had a distinctive appearance, even if it was a nod to the sixties; now he looked like just another smooth-faced pol with a razor cut.

Mauro knew that in order to run he had to try to change the subject from the FBI investigation and other implications that he cut too many ethical corners. Mauro had a loyal base, especially among Hispanics on the border, but raising money was going to be a significant problem. In late 1997 he looked at his meager campaign fund and decided he would put out a book that explained himself to the electorate. *Beaches, Bureaucrats and Big Oil* was a vanity book, and he hired a team of writers to help him get it out [one of the authors of this book was the editor], but he talked the stories through until he thought every line was right. He talked about public land, oil spills, and ships' dumping of garbage in the Gulf, the wisdom of Sam Houston and Bob Bullock. From Texas political writers he got the best press of his life. He embarked on a book tour, saying he was going to let people tell him whether he ought to run.

A year out from the election, he announced his candidacy, flying by private plane to several cities in the state, and it was a great day for him. But as the plane came back to Austin Mauro fell to brooding, thinking he would be met by the same cynical gang of reporters, sneering their unpleasant questions about his character. Instead there was a rowdy crowd of people holding up signs. For a few short weeks he could almost believe he had a chance.

Mauro had convincing polls showing that managed health care was suddenly a hot issue. He rolled the dice, spent what money he had, and went on TV with the issue, early in the summer of 1998. He looked good and sounded smart, yet the polls in favor of Bush didn't move. This time, Rove had Bush running on a single issue— the governor was determined that "social promotion" of educationally deficient grade-schoolers could no longer be allowed. Democrats heard it and gaped at each other. That was all Bush had?

It was all he needed. Rove didn't even have to put the headlines about Mauro and the FBI on the air. With speculation about the 2000 presidential campaign building, Bush's campaign was going to be heavily covered by the national media, just because of who he was. And because he spent $25 million on the campaign while his opponent spent less than $3 million.

Bush and Rove wanted to prove to the national audience that the candidate had strong support among Hispanics, so they hired a San Antonio consultant and spent more money on Spanish-language radio ads than Mauro could budget for his entire campaign. The Republicans went all-out to carry even traditionally Democratic, heavily Hispanic El Paso, and Mauro was obligated to fight desperately to salvage that outpost.

Rove consented to put Bush onstage with the Democrat in one debate. It took place in El Paso, which is in the mountain time zone, ensuring that in the state's major population centers it would be seen only by political junkies. The debate was one of the few times Bush's arrogance showed in public. He was inarticulate and barely civil, and he clearly lost the debate. But it was like Walter Mondale winning a presidential debate with Ronald Reagan in 1984—so what? Mauro would hold the line in El Paso, but just barely. Bush would get 49 percent.

The final twist of the knife was applied not by Rove, but by an irascible old man Rove had once terrified by sending an FBI agent after him. Or so Bob Bullock believed. In failing health—he had continued to chain-smoke, despite being diagnosed with lung cancer—Bullock had turned his attention to the construction of a new museum of Texas history (which would eventually be named after him) and sprucing up the State Cemetery, where he would soon be buried. Bullock was a complex character—the most fascinating Texas politician of his generation, if all the stories were to be sorted out and told. Who knows what drove him? "God bless Texas" was his signature signoff, and perhaps Bullock just believed one candidate would be better for Texas than the other, as he said. But Bush's election was a foregone conclusion, which made Bullock's endorsement of Bush over Mauro seem gratuitously cruel. Mauro had been Bullock's friend, his hand-picked protégé. Bullock had been godfather at the baptism of Mauro's little boy. He didn't have to break anybody's heart.

The Rove team had timed Bush's endorsements with a rhythm that Mauro later likened to Chinese water torture, culminating in the announcement that Bullock was endorsing George W. Bush. When it came, Mauro and his people were thunderstruck. They couldn't think of anything to say.

In the end, Mauro would barely break 40 percent, giving Bush what the commentators liked to call a record-setting mandate of approval. John Sharp would lose a cliffhanger to the Republican lieutenant governor candidate, who was none other than Karl Rove's discovery and sometime star, Rick Perry. Sharp blamed Mauro for his loss, saying his weakness brought the whole ticket down. But Bush didn't waste any time on a postmortem. As the frontrunner for the 2000 Republican presidential nomination, he had people to see and places to be.

8

The Yellow Rose Garden

"The Yellow Rose of Texas" is a rousing song that celebrates the apocryphal seduction of General Antonio López de Santa Anna by a mulatto named Emily West. During the final battle of Texas' war for independence from Mexico, she kept the general occupied in his tent while Sam Houston's soldiers swept down on the Mexican army camped on the banks of the San Jacinto River. George Bush's Yellow Rose Garden campaign was an equally spectacular act of seduction, planned and executed by Karl Rove. Rove kept the American public occupied with a parade of political functionaries arriving at the Governor's Mansion in Austin to endorse George W. Bush. While the public was engaged with four months of political theater, Rove raised money, home-schooled his candidate, and created the illusion that a thoughtful but reluctant governor of Texas was pondering the many requests that he run for president.

George W. Bush was ready for neither a presidential campaign nor the presidency when the Texas Legislature convened in January 1999. His most glaring weakness was a woeful ignorance about the world beyond Texas and Washington. Although he grew up in the shadow of a father who had been an ambassador to China, the U.S. delegate to the United Nations, and the director of the Central Intelligence Agency, Bush had never demonstrated a grasp of—or even an interest in—foreign affairs. In fact he hardly demonstrated much interest in domestic policy affairs in Texas, even after his upset victory over Ann Richards a little over four years earlier. None of this was a great liability in a state whose constitutional limitations on the governor's powers suited Bush's managerial style of governing.

But Bush was running for the presidency.

Rove conceived of a campaign that would turn his candidate's weakness into a strength—perhaps a virtue. He would keep the governor under wraps, while at the same time keeping him in the public eye. The message was simple. Bush had a great deal to say about the great national and international issues confronting the world's most powerful nation. And he would speak to all those issues.

But only after he fulfilled his responsibility to the voters in Texas, who elected him and depended on him to lead and govern. The January-to-June 1999 legislative session provided Bush a perfect opportunity to avoid exposure to the media. He would campaign only after the session ended, when the demands of office were not so urgent.

Rove knew, as did the Austin press corps, that Bush was not ready for prime time in January 1999. He was possessed of neither Bill Clinton's passion for policy nor Rove's voracious appetite for books. As governor, he had governed much as Ronald Reagan had as president—disengaged from the details of legislation and the history that informed it. Keeping Bush in the Governor's Mansion and his Capitol office was not a hastily conceived response to his lack of preparation; it was a carefully designed strategy. The extra study time was helpful. Yet Rove had already decided Bush would begin to "campaign" in the summer, shortly before the Iowa Straw Poll.

Nothing, in fact, had been hastily conceived.

In 1995, as he tells it, Rove decided that Bush would be "a fabulous candidate" for president—assuming he could govern as governor. So by 1999, Rove had been thinking about the campaign for five years and planning for three. The organizational plan for a national presidential campaign was in place long before legislators arrived in Austin that January. A year earlier Rove had set up campaign offices in each state, where staffs and directors could begin their work when the campaign required it.

Not only were campaign offices in place; the "spontaneous" national movement that would urge Bush to run was ready to move. In the fall of 1998 Rove had called Mississippi lawyer-lobbyist Haley Barbour. Barbour had served as the Republican Party's national chairman and was still a big player in the party. Rove pitched his plan to Barbour, as he would pitch it to others. He intended to persuade name Republicans, mostly in their forties and fifties, to join an exploratory committee. He wanted to avoid party leaders associated with Bush's father, because he wanted to make sure the committee looked like the future of the party—the next generation of Republican leaders, not its past.

It was a bold request. Rove was asking a party leader to commit to a presidential candidate more than a year before the first caucus or primary. Barbour said he would consider it. A one-on-one conversation with Bush himself finally closed the deal. (Bush may not have been openly working on Rove's quiet campaign to make him president, but he was not uninvolved.) While waiting for Barbour to come aboard, Rove had continued to work the phones, putting together a committee of Republican leaders willing to join the Bush team.

Republican governors also joined the effort. Montana's Marc Racicot had offered Bush his services in 1997 and Rove took him up on it. Michigan's John Engler was leaning on the Republican Governors' Association, playing on the political capital he had accrued while building the organization. As Bush was modestly suggesting he would consider running if there was support for his candidacy, Engler was urging governors to support Bush's candidacy—warning them not to wait until the train left the station. Or, as Rove would tell those who were not ready to commit: "Keep your powder dry." He wanted them to be ready to join the campaign when Bush announced

As the legislative session began, so did Rove's "spontaneous" groundswell of endorsements and public entreaties for Bush to run. Reporters were summoned to the south lawn of the mansion for carefully choreographed press conferences that would begin with a dignified procession of Republican governors emerging from the governor's residence. "This was neither requested nor authorized by Governor Bush," Mark Racicot said during one such event (which did raise the question about how they had gotten onto the grounds). Racicot was speaking for twelve governors who had traveled to Austin to pledge their support to Bush. He promised three more would soon follow. Another four governors would announce at a later date. With the governors came their statewide fundraising and campaign organizations. These events spared Bush from unseemly self-promotion and allowed him the time to attend to the responsibilities of the office. The endorsement parade charade was reminiscent of the "Chinese water torture" that Garry Mauro had experienced in his 1998 campaign against Bush, when endorsements were announced at regular intervals in the months before the election.

Also traveling to Austin were members of Congress, though Rove had to manage them with discretion, since Bush was running as an outsider, against Washington. Republican House Whip Tom DeLay's reputation for crude, muscular politics, for example, kept him off the Bush exploratory committee—although he was a dedicated supporter of the governor. His surrogate, the more benign deputy whip, Roy Blunt of Missouri, signed on in his stead. One of the messages Rove had Bush advancing was that government in Texas worked because of an absence of partisan politics (a claim utterly divorced from the reality of the political campaigns Rove had run since arriving in Texas twenty years earlier). To bring in Republican Party heavies from Washington risked association with what Bush called "the partisan politics of Washington, D.C." "I'm a uniter, not a divider," Bush would say (many, many times).

Foreign dignitaries were also paraded through the Governor's Mansion. On one February afternoon, William Hague, then head of Britain's Conservative Party, stood beaming as Bush predicted that the ineffectual Hague would become a prime minister as great as Winston Churchill (a notion that no doubt provoked a laugh riot at 10 Downing Street and in the editorial offices of even the most conservative Fleet Street dailies). On another afternoon, Bush introduced former Canadian Prime Minster Brian Mulroney in the House gallery. Another caller at the mansion was Qatar's foreign minister, Sheik Hamad bin Jassim bin Jabr al-Thani. The sheik was accompanied by his country's ambassador. "I get ambassadors that come all the time," Bush said. "This presidential speculation has seemed to have caused more governments to send their ambassadors my way. So I look forward to listening."

This was hardly an "A-List" of the world's leaders. Sheik Hamad was not a household name. Hague was so ineffective as a party leader that he is now banished from the leadership circles of his own party. And the six years Mulroney had been out of office were hardly sufficient for members of his Progressive Conservative Party to forget how badly he had governed. None of that mattered. Bush's greatest deficit, his slippery grasp of foreign policy issues, was being addressed by suggesting that the world's leaders were coming to Austin and that the governor was spending his time cloistered in the mansion with them—"listening," and therefore learning.

The south lawn of the Governor's Mansion (literalists should know there's no actual Yellow Rose Garden), and at times the mansion itself, were turned into sets for carefully choreographed events that were part of a campaign that was not supposed to exist. Yet the non-campaign was already more sophisticated than anything Bush's Republican rivals would field after their campaigns hit the road. In April, as the pace of events picked up, a Bush adviser who couldn't contain himself whispered to *The Weekly Standard's* Fred Barnes that Rove was the genius behind the throne: "He's been orchestrating all this. He's done a marvelous job, yet practically no one's accused him of manipulating it."

By that time, Rove had also orchestrated the campaign's first primary victory—the one Rove refers to as "the money primary"—which occurs before any formal declaration of candidacy. In that campaign Bush easily defeated John McCain, Gary Bauer, Lamar Alexander, Alan Keyes, Elizabeth Dole, and Pat Buchanan. It was a primary contest Rove began himself, before he brought in Donald L. Evans, Bush's old friend from the West Texas oilfields, to direct fundraising. While Evans would be the face on the fundraising campaign, Rove was the brain behind it. In an Austin office that one writer described as a virtual smoke-filled room, Rove made phone calls, sent faxes and at times dealt with as many as 300 e-mail messages a day. The man with the direct-mail experience and the best lists and Rolodex in the universe of Republican Party donors was reaching out of Austin and into their pockets. He had $7 million in the bank a month after Bush announced he might run—while Dan Quayle had raised $2 million, John McCain $1.6 million, and Christian conservative Gary Bauer $1.3 million. None of the others in the crowded Republican pack had reached the million-dollar mark. In fact, the money primary might have been over on March 31, 1999, the day Bush raised $2.3 million. On that day alone Bush brought in more than what John McCain had raised in all the previous months. By the end of June (when the Iowa Straw Poll was held), Rove and Evans had raised $36.4 million—more than the aggregate total raised by all of Bush's primary opponents. The only competition Rove faced in the money primary was the $38 million check Steve Forbes wrote to cover the cost of his own campaign—if that's considered fundraising. Though the visible political battle was yet to be joined, in reality the contest for the Republican presidential nomination was over before it began.

While the façade and south lawn of the mansion served as a stage for politicians expounding on reasons for endorsing Bush, other visitors were discreetly chauffeured in and out the back gate. Experts from across the country came to Austin to home-school Bush on the public policy issues he had to master before being exposed to the press and the public. Among them were the foreign policy scholar Condoleezza Rice; Herb Stein, who had chaired Richard Nixon's Council of Economic Advisers; former secretary of state George Shultz; and former Swedish Prime Minister Carl Bildt, who at the time was the UN special envoy to the Balkans.

North of the mansion, in the Capitol building, legislators faced enormous pressure to pass laws that would shore up Bush's conservative image. (If there was one pre-primary miscalculation Rove made, it was the assumption that the greatest threat Bush would face in the primary was political commentator Pat Buchanan.) The centerpiece of Bush's legislative agenda was the $2 billion tax cut, but there were other things to accomplish as well. A lax environmental law that locked the state out of compliance with federal EPA clean air mandates was passed to provide the campaign a model of cooperation with industry. A welfare bill with sanctions Democrats found too punitive was repeatedly reworked and referred to "the political office" watched over by Rove. Equally important was that certain legislation be stopped, such as a bill that would have prohibited the execution of mentally retarded individuals convicted of murder.

"You have to understand that Karl Rove believes that you govern to be reelected," said an Austin political consultant. "They were the most politically driven government we have ever had in Texas. And they are more politically driven now that they're in Washington."

As the pre-campaign grew into a campaign, Rove moved from the periphery of campaign events closer to the candidate at the center of the stage. He was more available than he had previously been, talking more to reporters, arguing the significance of polling trends, making predictions, offering reporters more than they asked for.

Bush would win the nomination, he said, because the Haley Barbours of the party, and 114 U.S. House members, and fourteen U.S. Senators, and a substantial majority of Republican governors had endorsed him. He was the candidate of the establishment, and he was ahead by more than ten points in the polls. Historically, any candidate who combined those two factors won the nomination. It was one of many predictors Rove would refer to.

When the media outlets handicapping the race got it wrong, Rove called them on it. "*Newsweek*'s bullshit," he told Austin reporter Robert Bryce in response to a question at the end of one press conference about the newsweekly's prediction that Bush was at a disadvantage in the general election. In less than a minute, Rove ran the numbers on how Bush would beat Gore in the Electoral College. "It's a rather simple equation," Rove said. "One hundred, 114, twelve, equals forty-four . . . There are 100 Electoral College votes between the Sierra Nevadas and the Missouri River—from Idaho to North Dakota and from Arizona to Texas and everything in between plus Alaska," Rove said. And all are in "good shape for Bush. Solid. In fact they [the Gore campaign] are only making a play for one of those states.

"Take 114 in the South, not including Tennessee. And they are only playing essentially for three of those states: Louisiana, Arkansas, and Florida. But we are in good shape in all three of those. Indiana gives us twelve more. That gets us to 226. That leaves forty-four more to go.

"We've got to put forty-four more to go—out of four in Maine, four in New Hampshire, three in Delaware, twenty-three in Pennsylvania, twenty-one in Ohio, eighteen in Michigan, eleven in Wisconsin, eleven in Missouri, twenty-two in Illinois, seven in Iowa, eleven in Washington state, seven in Oregon," Rove said. "We have to find forty-four out of that . . . what is it, 119? [It's 142.] And we have thirty-two of them locked up. Maybe thirty-six."

Bryce walked away a believer—although he would later recall Rove's response—"No. No. No. No. Not going to happen!"—when he said his reading of the electoral map suggested that Gore could win the popular vote and lose in the Electoral College. There were very few instances when Rove did not have an answer that stated or implied the inevitability of the Bush presidency.

In March 1999 Bush told Rove he had to sell his consulting firm if he wanted to be a part of the campaign. Rove's sister, Reba Hammond, said her family was surprised that Bush—who was being made enormously wealthy by the sale of the Texas Rangers baseball team and its taxpayer-financed stadium—made her brother sell the company he had worked so hard to build. "We all thought it was kind of odd," she said. "Why didn't he just take a sabbatical? And he told us he didn't sell it for quite the price he wanted." A past employee of the consulting business said that Rove told him Bush ordered the sale because he "wanted 120 percent of his attention. He wanted him full-time—day and night."

Rove was already fully engaged. For the past two years he had talked to Bush at least twice a day. With the sale of Karl Rove + Company, not only was he Bush's full-time employee; he was in full control of the campaign. The guy who had once handed the family car keys to a young George W. Bush was now in the driver's seat.

The fights in Texas, the bugging of the Clements campaign, the tabloid that recycled the story of Mark White's college DWI—they all seemed like the script from another play. Rove and his wife Darby, a graphic designer at his company, whom he had married in 1986, had bought and remodeled a charming home that had once been a farmhouse. Their son Andrew had been born in 1989, but in school the little boy had some learning difficulties, and the genius dad paid close attention to his son's schooling, helping him get over that hump. Then Rove was staggered a few years later when Darby was diagnosed with breast cancer. It was a terrifying time in their lives, but they had gotten through it—and now her health was good. Nearing fifty, Rove was no longer the perennial College Republican. He had grown up, just as the youthful wildseed George W. Bush had grown up.

Though Bush demanded full-time attention, it's a measure of Rove's enormous energy that during that run-up to 2002 he found time to teach a popular course on politics at the University of Texas' LBJ School of Public Affairs—a graduate program for aspiring bureaucrats. Rove had half a dozen colleges on his transcript by now, but he still did not have a bachelor's degree, and it bothered him. While finishing off the last of the state's Democrats and preparing to take on the daunting task of running a presidential campaign, he enrolled in a Ph.D. program in the university's first-rate history department. By the time he would arrive in Washington in 2001, the movers would dolly out 148 boxes of books. Most of them were about politics.

From the governor's office and the formative presidential campaign there were stories that Bush would indulge great yawns when Rove launched into one of his political monologues. "Oh, very nice point, Karl," Bush would snicker when he thought a Rove remark or proposal was off the wall. A reporter asked a Bush team insider how sensitive Rove was to these jibes. "I don't know. He takes some rough ones." In Bush's management style, what mattered was keeping all disagreement inside the tent. There was just one boss and candidate—just one star—and everyone on the team was expected to conform to his or her roles. Sometimes Rove was tempted to wax verbose and accept credit that everyone in Austin knew he deserved. According to the *Dallas Morning News*, on one occasion Bush saw some reporters gathered around his adviser and groused: "Is the Rove news conference over?" Chastened, Rove moved away from them. Darby Rove said she believed her husband's friendship with Bush was more philosophical than personal. She said Karl "has hundreds of friends and no one he's intimate with" outside their small family. As the presidential race took form, Rove told another Texas newspaper: "I have no other persona other than Bush."

Even if Bush sometimes poked fun at Rove's eggheadedness, he had to appreciate that Rove's study of politics had made him a master of political narrative. What Rove was doing, as Bush used the Legislature as a pretext to stay in Austin, was creating a story line. The elements of the story included a noble governor who wouldn't abandon his charge until it was complete, the leaders of a political party who wouldn't rest until the governor accepted the call to run for the presidency, financial backers willing to invest in the candidacy, and the inevitability of Bush's election.

It was a political narrative with its own historical antecedent. The Bush campaign was a modern-day version of the campaign of President William McKinley a century earlier. Like Bush, McKinley had been elected to a statewide office limited in its power by constitutional restraints. Also like Bush, McKinley had campaigned in 1896 from the Governor's Mansion, in his case in Ohio. As it developed, Bush's Yellow Rose Garden Campaign became more and more like McKinley's "Front Porch Campaign."

That, at least, was the narrative Rove imposed on it.

There were other historical parallels beyond the porch. McKinley tried to redefine the Republican Party, much as Rove thought he and Bush were doing in their appeal to working-class voters and immigrants. McKinley also faced a Republican Party that was threatened by internal divisions as treacherous as those faced by the modern party, as Christian social conservatives often find themselves at odds with economic conservatives. And McKinley's campaign flowed out of Ohio on a river of money.

In his graduate studies, Rove had naturally focused on Republican politics. He had an interest in and an admiration for Wendell Willkie, whom Franklin D. Roosevelt overwhelmed in 1940. Then he told two distinguished historians on the faculty, Lewis Gould and Robert Divine, that he wanted to set the record straight on the Republican race and national convention of 1896. Rather than becoming a Willkie revisionist, he would resurrect the career of William McKinley.

Rove and his young son spent many nights at the university library, photocopying documents and hauling piles of books to a carrel. Without a bachelor's degree, Rove did not have all the prerequisites for the doctoral quest, of course. The university required him to take an undergraduate course that demonstrated his writing ability, which by all accounts is considerable. He worked hard for a semester, at which point the university discovered that the course he had taken was no longer in the catalogue. His work was all for naught; if he wanted to keep going, he had to take another course of similar description. Incredibly, instead of tongue-lashing some tenure-cushioned dean as he had done to reporters who had crossed Bush, Rove signed up for the course.

After reading all the books and papers he could find, Rove concluded that William McKinley was the most underrated American president. The ballyhooed Texan political strategist Mark Hanna, who was to McKinley as Rove was to Bush, was little more than a fundraiser. The unknown geniuses of the McKinley campaign were two politicos in their thirties. One, Charles Dawes, would rise to be a vice president and ambassador to Great Britain and would win a Nobel Peace Prize. The other was Theodore Roosevelt.

Rove's love of history was evident in the enthusiasm with which he reconstructed the past, using the present tense to do so. Theodore Roosevelt, Rove would enthuse, has the most fabulous job in the world. He's police commissioner of New York. A year later, 1896, he hates it. He backs the wrong candidate for the Republican presidential nomination. He writes a wonderful letter to his sister saying "McKinley, I think he's a dolt. You know, he's just not up to it." And yet by the end of the campaign, Roosevelt has ridden a train across the country to campaign for McKinley. He has enthusiastically campaigned for his candidacy and delivered two important speeches for him before crowds of tens of thousands of people. At the end of the campaign Roosevelt is rescued from obscurity by being rewarded with the job that vaults him into his future: assistant secretary of the Navy.

How could this relic of presidential history be germane to a race that would unfold 104 years later?

"Look," Rove would explain, "the 1896 thing was interesting

only because it represented the kind of election this might be. That is to say, an election [in] which each party's agendas were largely irrelevant or in danger of becoming irrelevant, in which each party had the responsibility of trying to come to cope with a changed circumstance of the country, changed demography, changed economy, changed world situation, changed nature of the party, and the declining power of each party's elite. In the case of McKinley, all the people who fought in the Civil War were dying off, and this was going to be the last election—in fact, it was one election past the point at which the parties could fight on the slogans from the 1860s. No longer could you say 'states' rights' as a Democrat and 'vote as you fought' if you were a Republican.

"So I don't want to carry the analogy too far. But it did allow us to sort of . . . we did steal most prominently the idea of the front porch campaign from it. Only we applied it to the primary, not to the general."

To Rove, history is a flowing continuum, and it's instructive. Like all history buffs, he also enjoys a good yarn. He developed a great admiration for Teddy Roosevelt's virility and decisiveness, as well as for the assassinated president he succeeded. After he himself was one of its occupants, Rove loved to tell the story of how the West Wing of the White House came about. The center of the executive branch needed more office space, and Roosevelt was hectoring the architects, builders, and landscapers to get the project done quickly. Over the years glass conservatories had been erected around the White House, Rove would say, beaming. "People liked to see orange trees growing, that sort of thing. Roosevelt's wife found out they were going to take out the conservatories, and she told the architect, 'You can't do that.'"

Rove paused, then delivered the punch line: Roosevelt turned to the architect and ordered, "Smash the glass houses!" The historian and strategist smiled, then explained that Roosevelt's decisiveness had come at a cost. The builders, hurried by executive fiat, had done shoddy work, and after TR left office, the new addition had to be torn down and rebuilt. Rove summarized the incident with a certain bemusement:

"He got his way, but they had to clean up after him."

9

Firewall

Rove's strategy for taking the Republican nomination read like some inscrutable Taoist treatise: First, align the full power and majesty of the Republican establishment behind your candidate. Then sell him to voters as an outsider eager to upend the status quo.

Both prongs of the plan were necessary. As had been the case in George W. Bush's business career, one of the governor's biggest assets was his ability to attract the support of the wealthy and powerful to enterprises that might seem chancy to the casual onlooker. By the end of June—less than three weeks after he announced his candidacy—his campaign had raised $36.4 million. The best way to convince voters—and, more importantly, contributors—of his viability was to line up the big guns before anyone had a chance to ask questions, so that to question Bush was to question the judgment of his august supporters.

The fundraising wasn't the half of it. Rove was everywhere, setting up campaign headquarters in all fifty states, securing further endorsements, and even buying up potentially embarrassing Web site names like www.georgebushsucks.net and connecting them to the campaign's home page. From the beginning, it was a national campaign, and Rove oversaw every aspect of it. If the devil is in the details, he had found Karl Rove waiting to greet him when he got there.

But given Bush's decidedly local résumé—more than one critic was calling him the least qualified presidential candidate of modern times, and unflattering comparisons to Warren G. Harding were not uncommon—Rove had almost no choice but to run him as an outsider. An electorate fatigued by Bill Clinton's endless dance of equivocation and triangulation (and the virulent Republican reactions it provoked) was ripe for promises to "change the tone in Washington." The pledge was cast in political terms, but the moral implications were clear. Clinton had done Bush a tremendous favor by creating a political climate in which "experience" was a dirty word, or at least tainted by association.

Rove had set up most of the first part of his plan before Bush had even announced his candidacy. Now he set about introducing Bush to the people who at some point would actually have to vote for him. The candidate began to appear with increasing frequency in the states that would determine the frontrunners as the primary season got underway: Iowa, where the first party caucuses would be held in January, and New Hampshire and South Carolina, the sites of early primaries.

The idea was to appear presidential, with the dual purpose of intimidating Bush's challengers and—on some symbolic level—assuaging doubts about his fitness for the office. One staffer recalled the effect the campaign had on the communities through which it passed: "Bush—like most governors—traveled with security, which meant motorcades, cops, flashing lights; and there were always scores of press in pursuit. It was an impressive show that swept people up in its excitement. . . . When it worked, it was like a shadow government in motion. We'd hit a town and it was like nothing they'd ever seen." Bush would emerge from a car, appear before an enormous crowd, uncan his remarks, and disappear back into his motorized phalanx. While this approach minimized the retail politicking that had helped to make him popular in Texas, it also minimized the likelihood of the embarrassing verbal slips he was prone to and ensured that he wouldn't have to deal with the press, a chore he openly disliked, any more than necessary.

It helped that there wasn't much in the way of competition. Of the candidates who were already seeking the Republican nomination by the time Bush entered the race, only self-declared Christian candidate and former Reagan aide Gary Bauer could be considered a fresh face, politically speaking. The others—publishing heir Steve Forbes, Utah Senator Orrin Hatch, former Vice President Dan Quayle, commentator Pat Buchanan, former Tennessee governor Lamar Alexander—were all damaged goods to one extent or another, having attempted the race before and been squelched early on in the process. (They would be joined in September by Alan Keyes, a pro-life candidate whose unpredictable swings between riveting oratory and paranoid ranting earned him the eternal gratitude of a stultified press corps.)

They were all toast, and Rove knew it. His strategy of frontloading the money and endorsements had paid off handsomely, and although Bush would be obligated to go through the motions of a few debates to avoid the appearance of arrogance, it looked like he was on his way to the nomination without having to get out of his car too often. Rove and Karen Hughes had already begun the lengthy process of publicly lowering expectations for the debates, painting the governor as more of a big-picture kind of guy than a big-words kind of guy, an assessment that anyone who'd ever heard him talk found at least partly credible.

On September 27, one final candidate formally entered the race. Senator John McCain of Arizona did not mention the heir-presumptive to the Republican nomination once during his announcement, but every other sentence was an implied reproach to Bush: "There comes a time when our nation's leader can no longer rely on briefing books and talking points," he said. "[The president] is alone in a dark room when the casualty lists come in. I'm not afraid of that burden. I know both the blessing and price of freedom."

McCain's very existence was also an implied reproach to Bush. A Navy pilot who had been shot down over Vietnam, McCain had been held as a POW for five and a half years, during which time he was tortured so severely that thirty years later he still walked with a pronounced limp and was incapable of lifting his arms high enough to comb his own hair. McCain, whose father and grandfather were four-star admirals, was offered early release by his captors, who seemed to think that sending the pilot they called "The Crown Prince" home would make good propaganda material. Citing the military Code of Conduct, which specifies that prisoners must be released in the order they were captured, McCain repeatedly refused early release, and was tortured further for his refusal. He was finally released in 1972, the same year that Bush entered the Texas National Guard.

McCain went on to become a senator from Arizona in the Goldwater conservative mold, though with a bent toward contrariness, as when he took on his own party establishment to battle for campaign finance reform, another linchpin of his campaign: "When our government has been taken from us by the special interests, the big-dollar donors, pride is lost to shame," he said in his announcement. Again, he didn't mention Bush by name. He didn't need to. The governor's fundraising prowess was one of the few things most Americans knew about him.

With McCain in the race, Bush's piles of green suddenly took on a sinister tint. Bush was running as an outsider, not as big money incarnate, but now money was an issue, right up there with his fitness to govern. And the issue was being raised by someone else with just as much claim, if not more, to the outsider tag. Just by declaring his candidacy, McCain was calling into question some of the basic premises of the Bush run.

For Rove, who had never displayed any particular talent for separating the personal from the political, the insurgency was particularly galling. McCain's campaign was being run by a Texas A&M grad named John Weaver, with whom Rove had worked years before, first for Bill Clements in 1986 and then on George Bush's presidential run in 1988. Something had happened between them—a dispute over payment, it was said—and the resulting split was deep and bitter.

The brilliant and mercurial Weaver, nine years Rove's junior, had gone on to become the state party's executive director before facing off against Rove in the 1993 special election to fill Lloyd Bentsen's Senate seat when Bentsen was named Secretary of the Treasury. Rove had won that one, but hadn't stopped there, according to the Weaver camp, who accused him of spreading rumors about Weaver that made it harder and harder for him to find work. Rove's adherents rejoined that Weaver just couldn't handle being everyone's second choice.

Whatever had happened, it was apparently time for a grudge match, and grudge was the operative word. "These guys absolutely detest each other," said a Republican consultant who knew both. "It's as much personal—maybe more—as it is professional." Weaver, who shared his employer's short fuse and who was prone to dark moods—McCain's ironic nickname for him was "Sunny"— was open in his disdain for the Bush campaign, audibly snorting with derision when the governor stumbled during debates. The news that Bush was presidential timber was apparently late in getting to the McCain camp.

Bush's huge monetary advantage over McCain meant that the upstart campaign was forced to operate in a very different fashion from Rove's stately march to victory. McCain later admitted that it was less tactical brilliance than sheer necessity that led him to give reporters unprecedented access, but for whatever reasons it quickly became his hallmark. McCain would sit in a red leather swivel chair at the rear of his bus, dubbed the Straight Talk Express, and talk to reporters for hours at a time with a candor previously unheard of in political campaigns.

McCain's irreverence and forthrightness—a typical comment began with the phrase "One of the many reasons I hate the French . . . "—did not disappear when he was in front of voters. Constrained by their relatively limited resources, McCain and Weaver had written off the Iowa caucuses, which would yield no delegates, and devoted their attention to New Hampshire, barnstorming the state in a series of more than a hundred "town meetings," at which McCain would take any question from whoever showed up. It was at such a meeting in Portsmouth that he announced that as president he would consider shutting down the Portsmouth Naval Base, a major local employer. "I told you when I started this campaign that I would tell you things you don't want to hear," he said.

Judging from the polls, most voters seemed to agree with Bob Dole, who remarked about his fellow senator that if you spend five and a half years in a box, you get to say anything you want. Drawn by his tale of personal heroism (his autobiography, *Faith of My Fathers*, was #2 on the *New York Times* bestseller list), crowds stayed to listen to his pleas for campaign finance reform and honest government. The fact that some of them were disaffected Democrats brought little cheer to the Bush campaign.

Given that McCain was not attacking Bush directly, there was little Rove could legitimately do but bide his time and hope for McCain to scuttle his own boat with a temper tantrum or particularly impolitic remark. But a December incident involving Rove led some reporters to believe that not everyone at headquarters was sitting on their hands.

Someone had started floating rumors that McCain was mentally unstable as a result of being tortured in Vietnam, and that the pressure of the presidency might cause him to snap. Wayne Slater, a reporter for the *Dallas Morning News*, wrote a piece ruminating about the origin of the whispering campaign in which he recounted a number of questionable practices that had been attributed to Rove over the years: teaching college Republicans dirty tricks; circulating a mock newspaper that featured a story about Mark White's drinking and driving when he was a college student; spreading stories about Jim Hightower's alleged role in a contribution kickback scheme; and alerting the press to the fact that Lena Guerrero had lied about graduating from college—all of which had been reported or attributed elsewhere. Slater also reported that candidates Gary Bauer and Steve Forbes had fingered the Bushies as the McCain rumormongers.

In early December, Rove—who had not returned Slater's phone calls about the story—confronted the reporter in the New Hampshire airport, poking a finger into his chest and saying, "You broke the rules!" The outburst had an effect that Rove had perhaps not reckoned on. A reporter who was present said that as a result of the incident, "everyone on the campaign charter concluded that Rove was responsible for the rumors about McCain."

But whoever was responsible was no doubt disappointed by the results. On the evening of February 1, the Bush team sank into despondency as they watched McCain's lead assume embarrassing proportions—Bush would eventually trail him by 18 percentage points—while McCain himself seemed unable to register the information until his aide and co-author Mark Slater said "You could be president." Turning to Weaver, McCain barked, "A fine mess you've gotten me into!"

It was a mess that Rove was determined to get him out of. Stung by McCain's win—and by the avalanche of stories on how the Bush juggernaut had sprung a leak—he turned his attention to the next primary, in South Carolina, and what he saw there gave him hope.

The South Carolina primary had a reputation as a Republican "firewall"—a quick slapdown for insurgent candidates who had managed to pick up steam in Iowa and New Hampshire. The firewall concept, like so much of modern political warfare, was originally the handiwork of Rove's mentor Lee Atwater. It was in the 1988 presidential campaign that Atwater had first correctly judged that South Carolina's rigidly conservative political hierarchy would turn out for the Republican establishment's candidate, then as in

2000 named George Bush. After all, this was a state that had continued to send the doddering Strom Thurmond to Washington long past the point when such an exercise made any political sense.

After a life spent elevating national politics to the level of those in South Carolina, on his deathbed Atwater supposedly renounced the type of negative campaign he had made the new gold standard in politics, an admirable gesture that had little or no effect on the 2000 Republican primary.

Coming off a huge poll bounce as a result of New Hampshire, McCain proceeded to make a series of mistakes, at least in the context of South Carolina politics. He made comments that hurt him with Confederate flag supporters, the religious right, and pro-life groups—the last even though his pro-life voting record was impeccable—while Bush and Rove swiped a page from his book and started touting the governor as a "reformer with results." Within days, voters had started identifying Bush, rather than McCain, as the reformer.

Then McCain said something about Bush that was apparently unforgivable, even in the rough-and-tumble of South Carolina politics: He accused him of "twisting the truth like Clinton."

To a South Carolina Republican, this was filth tantamount to impugning someone's mother, and the Bush campaign responded with appropriate outrage. Mark McKinnon was now Bush's media maven, and the speed with which he and Rove got a response on the air was decisive. "That commercial McKinnon and those guys cut was the Godzilla judo flip," says Trey Walker, who was McCain's national field director. "McCain's momentum had already started to evaporate, and that just stopped him dead." The response ad, which featured a stern Bush inveighing against McCain, served two purposes: It answered the first ad, and it cemented in voters' minds the idea that McCain was the one using negative ads, an impression that McCain inadvertently confirmed when, a week before the end of the campaign, he promised to *stop* running negative ads.

Seasoned watchers of South Carolina politics seem to agree that McCain never had a chance, given his own gaffes and the overwhelming support of the state's Republican establishment for Bush. And as Walker points out, the Bush campaign hit their marks this time: "It was pretty simple what they needed to do, and they executed it flawlessly. And that was to make John McCain unacceptable to a large segment of conservative South Carolina voters."

But the question that lingers—as it seems to linger whenever Karl Rove is calling the shots—is why the campaign got as nasty as it did, when by all accounts Bush could have won anyway. Because somehow—although nobody will take responsibility—it got incredibly nasty. "I have worked on hundreds of campaigns in South Carolina," says Michael Graham, a conservative writer and radio host who at the time had a show in Charleston, "and I've never seen anything as ugly as that campaign. It was 100 percent 'John McCain sucks.' Bush never said 'Here's why you should vote for me.'"

This time, instead of one rumor about McCain, there were scores. McCain was gay. McCain had fathered an illegitimate child with a North Vietnamese woman, which was why he had gotten special treatment from the Viet Cong. McCain had a black daughter. (McCain and his wife, Cindy, have an adopted daughter from Bangladesh.) McCain voted for the largest tax increase ever. McCain's wife stole prescription drugs from a charity and abused them while she was supposedly caring for their four children. McCain was pro-abortion. McCain left his crippled first wife. McCain was a liar, a cheat, and a fraud.

These canards were repeated on handbills, in phone calls, in push polls, on the radio, in conversation. "I've seen dirty politics, but I've never seen a rumor campaign like this," said Terry Haskins, the speaker pro tem of the South Carolina House of Representatives and a McCain supporter. "It's a vile attempt to destroy a man's reputation just to win an election, and I know it's organized because none of these rumors existed until the day after New Hampshire." Over a ten-day period, McCain's unfavorability rating went from 4 percent to 18 percent, while Bush's dropped from 26 percent to 20 percent.

On February 12, a week before the election, Bush had been caught by a C-SPAN camera talking to State Senator Mike Fair, though neither man apparently knew they were being watched.

"You haven't even hit his soft spots," said Fair, referring to McCain.

"I know," Bush replied. "I'm going to."

"Well they need to be, somebody does, anyway," Fair said.

"I agree," Bush said, adding, "I'm not going to do it on TV."

PART 3

THE MAN
WITH THE PLAN

10

A Matter of the Numbers

George W. Bush's relationship with John McCain was damaged forever in South Carolina, and the two men's staffs were doomed to a future of mutual loathing. But if the cost of the victory was high, so were its rewards. The advantages in fundraising, party endorsements and grassroots organizing that Rove and the old Bush family network had assembled had indeed proved to be the "firewall" that Bush needed. The polls closed at 7:00 PM in South Carolina, and a couple of minutes later McCain phoned Bush, who was sitting in his fifth-floor suite in the Columbia Sheraton Hotel, to concede the state. Later, in his concession speech to supporters, McCain would say, apparently referring to the tactics that had been used against him, "I want the presidency in the best way, not the worst way."

In his own hotel room, Karl Rove was already planning a general election campaign. Michigan was only three days away. There, despite Republican governor John Engler's vow to use his political organization to push Bush over the top, McCain was running strong. In fact, McCain would win Michigan as well as his home base of Arizona on February 22. But the nomination was all but over anyway. It was a matter of the numbers, something that would appeal to Bush, a man who loves baseball in part because of the order imposed on the sport by its vast array of statistics. Rove is not a baseball fan, but he could rattle off the stats that made Bush's presidential nomination all but inevitable: As the 2000 primary season began, Bush had more cash on hand than McCain, Gore and Bill Bradley combined. In endorsements, McCain had seven members of the House of Representatives; Bush had 175. In the Senate, where McCain served, only four of the war hero's colleagues had signed onto "The Straight Talk Express." Bush had thirty-seven Republican senators backing him.

A look at the nominating calendar showed why such figures were so significant. From that point on it was truly a national campaign, requiring a national organization. McCain's great asset was the McCain persona itself: he was drawing big, enthusiastic crowds that fed off his energy. Bush's campaign, by contrast, was built on his organization, meaning that the governors, senators, and other prominent Republicans backing him could serve as his surrogates, not only speaking on his behalf, but mobilizing their ground troops to get out the vote. This advantage kicked in almost immediately. The Bush campaign also had enough money to run television spots anywhere—and everywhere. Five days after Michigan came contests in American Samoa, Guam, the Virgin Islands, and Puerto Rico, with twenty-six delegates among them. Three days later, on February 29, some ninety-six delegates were up for grabs in North Dakota, Virginia, and Washington. Super Tuesday, on March 7, entailed competing in eleven states simultaneously, including five in New England, one in the deep South (Georgia), three in the Midwest (Ohio, Missouri, and Minnesota) and the bi-coastal megastates New York and California. A week after that came what amounted to a Southern regional primary, with six primaries the length of Dixie, from Florida to Texas. McCain's campaign was built on his personality, but he couldn't be more than one place at a time to showcase it. Bush's campaign was built on his organization, which in those early days functioned just as well without him, sometimes better.

Bush's public comments indicated that he, as well as Rove, was now looking ahead to a general-election campaign. "South Carolina has spoken—and tonight there are only 263 days more to the end of Clinton-Gore," Bush told a happy crowd in the Sheraton ballroom shortly after 9:00 PM. "My reform agenda stands in stark contrast to the current administration."

To counter McCain, Rove and Karen Hughes had wanted Bush to use the word "reform" everywhere he went in South Carolina. The candidate had mastered his lines so well that he couldn't stop. He mentioned "reform" a half-dozen times in his brief victory speech, at one point even lapsing into using the campaign slogan in the third person, telling his loyalists that the South Carolina election returns constituted "the victory of a message that is conservative and compassionate" and "the victory of a messenger who is a reformer with results." In New Hampshire, the late-deciding voters had almost all broken for McCain. In South Carolina, among a more conservative electorate and aided by McCain's decision to pull all negative spots in the last days of the primary, very nearly the opposite had occurred.

Rove's take was that Bush's breakthrough in South Carolina was due to a return to the strategies they had used in the 1994 governor's race. Complementing the attack ads on McCain was Bush's campaign trail demeanor, which was relentlessly assertive, but not in a way that turned voters off. In fact, exit polls showed that slightly more than half of South Carolina's voters believed McCain had run a more negative campaign than Bush. Moreover, the exit polls showed they had blunted, if not co-opted, McCain's reform message in their ads hammering away at McCain's own fundraising practices. This was possible, Rove declared, because Bush had been specific in detailing the reforms he wanted to make. "Bush won this because of a positive message," Rove said. "We run by uniting the Republican Party."

McCain's camp had a different take on what had happened in South Carolina. "They were able to throw a thousand axes through the air and we were only able to fend off so many," countered John Weaver. "That won't happen again."

Rove and Bush had already made the decision to change tactics, but not because they feared a stronger McCain response. After South Carolina it wasn't primarily about McCain for them. It was about Al Gore—and Bill Clinton. The voters' reaction against McCain for running ads comparing Bush to Clinton had bolstered Team Bush's conviction that Clinton was an asset to them, one that would galvanize conservative voters to vote against Clinton's vice president. At the same time, the exigencies of winning in South Carolina had forced Bush too far to the right—not where he wanted to be during the convention season or the general election campaign. Democrats tracked this development with obvious delight. Speaking of McCain as well as Bush, Gore noted wryly in remarks to the reporters traveling with him, "It's pretty clear that they have done a lot of damage to one another." Out in Los Angeles, Bill Carrick, a Democratic operative advising Gore, assured Democrats that the

George W. Bush on display in South Carolina would not play in California—a state Rove wanted to contest in November. Carrick, a South Carolina native who got started in politics by going up against Lee Atwater, told *Los Angeles Times* political writer Mark Barabak that Rove was running "a situational ethics sort of campaign. The thinking was, do whatever . . . to get out of South Carolina with a victory, then clean up the mess afterward."

For the Bush campaign the first step in that process was to atone with Roman Catholic voters—and Catholic Republican office holders—offended by Bush's February 2 campaign event at Bob Jones University, whose founder forbade inter-racial dating and once characterized Catholicism as "a Satanic cult." Bush had protested that an appearance at the school had generally been considered obligatory for GOP presidential candidates and that, in any event, he'd in no way associated himself with Jones' antediluvian views on matters of race and religion. Bush's protestations were accurate, but they weren't getting him anywhere, which he and Rove soon realized. A series of editorials in large newspapers in the primary states still in play called on Bush to do more. On February 27, he did. In a two-pronged chess move, the campaign released a contrite letter the governor had sent to New York Cardinal John O'Connor while Bush himself held a press conference in Austin to apologize personally. "On reflection, I should have been more clear in disassociating myself from anti-Catholic sentiments and racial prejudice," Bush said in the letter to O'Connor. "It was a missed opportunity, causing needless offense, which I deeply regret."

Bush aides asserted that the letter to O'Connor was initially intended to remain private, but it's clear from the calendar (the New York primary was approaching) and the wording of the letter that it was intended for a wider audience. "I want to erase any doubts about my views and values," Bush wrote. "As a public official, I take seriously my duty to encourage tolerance and respect for the religious views of others. As a Christian, I see Catholics as my brothers and sisters in Christ, sharing the same ancient creed and core beliefs. And, as you know, my own brother and sister-in-law are both Catholics."

The letter also had a tone of being aggrieved as well. "What no American should expect—and what I will not tolerate—is guilt by association," Bush added. "This is why I am offended by any suggestion that I tolerate anti-Catholic bigotry—and resent any attempt to create that impression."

Bush made the same point in Austin. Although he began by saying, "I make no excuses. I had an opportunity and missed it," Bush also went on the offensive. Lyndon Johnson, another Texan, once said, "If you're covering your ass, you're losing your ass," and George W. Bush had no intention of losing his. He expressed resentment that McCain's forces had been exploiting the Bob Jones University speech with Catholics, saying he'd been "slandered" by McCain. Bush went further, essentially calling McCain, who'd denied that his campaign had been using the matter in its phone bank work, a liar.

"I'm very disappointed in the senator," Bush said. "It was clear that he looked you in the press corps in the eye and did not tell the truth."

This time it was not the Bush camp with the credibility problem. After the campaign shifted to Michigan, it soon became evident what Rove nemesis John Weaver had meant by his dark hints that the McCainiacs wouldn't be caught flat-footed again. There was no more Mr. Nice Guy from McCain. Telephone calls to Michigan households from callers who identified themselves as being associated with something called "Catholic Voter Alert," read from a script saying that because of Bush's silence about "Bob Jones' anti-Catholic bigotry many Michigan Catholics now support John McCain for president." McCain initially denied that his campaign had anything to do with the calls when in fact, "Catholic Voter Alert" had been paid for by the McCain campaign. McCain admitted to *The New York Times* that he'd personally approved the script. McCain attempted to explain away his denial by quibbling with the wording of the question in his earlier denial. His performance disillusioned even some of the reporters aboard "Straight Talk Express." Rove and Bush pounced quickly.

"That's not plain talk, that's parsed talk," Bush said on February 27, after his campaign plane landed in Seattle. "This is a man who said, 'I'm going to tell the truth and run a positive campaign.' If the facts are what they are, it sounds like he might have violated both."

On the Sunday talk shows, Rove was even more blunt. In a confrontation with former Senator Warren Rudman, a McCain loyalist, Rove accused McCain of "reprehensible" conduct. "Now, right now, he's running a television ad right now saying: 'I'll always tell you the truth.' I guess the real question is, when is he going to *start* telling us the truth?" Rove said. "He had a sleazy, anonymous smear phone campaign in Michigan that only now is being acknowledged."

McCain ended up winning Michigan, but it was far more costly than Bush's win in South Carolina. Out-organized, out-financed and with little in the way of support from the GOP establishment,

McCain's insurgency was built on his credibility and charisma. One of those was diminished now, and Rove knew that the Republican nomination was Bush's for the taking.

By Super Tuesday, March 7, the Bush campaign's aura of inevitability was restored. *The New York Times*' Melinda Henneberger, who provided some of the most telling insights of Rove, was allowed to follow him through the afternoon of triumph. With perhaps more than the usual pleasure of his competitive juices, Rove called Bush from Austin to share the good news coming from the exit polls and to gloat over the "meltdown" of the McCain candidacy.

"It's not pretty, they say," he told Bush. "It's not pretty how the numbers are being received. [McCain is] going to Arizona, and the scuttlebutt is he's going to his cabin and nobody thinks he can continue. Yeah, recriminations, finger-pointing. . . . No, over there. Oh, big time. It's unbelievable." Rove went on to trash a major McCain adviser, Rick Davis. Davis' consulting firm had once accepted as clients Imelda Marcos and the nation of Nigeria. "Yeah, he is a bad guy," Rove assured the governor. "This guy was a lobbyist for Imelda Marcos and General Abacha of Nigeria! Just the consummate inside-D.C. thug. He needs adult supervision."

Later, Bush campaign staff and volunteers gathered at the posh Four Seasons hotel to celebrate the Super Tuesday results, results that would put them over the top in securing the Republican nomination. According to the *Times*, Karen Hughes burst into the suite as Rove was getting off the phone with the governor. He told her he just wanted to "get New York over with so we can go home."

"Go home?" Hughes yelled. "I want to celebrate."

Later, as Rove walked into the victory celebration, someone called out: "The king has arrived!" A Texas magazine publisher knelt before Rove and pretended to kiss his ring. Rove turned, bent over, and raised his jacket, the message being: Kiss My Ass. The reporter from New York asked Rove if he was enjoying himself. "Boring, man, boring!" he yelled. In his moment of national arrival he seemed edgy and distant.

Darby Rove later explained her husband's behavior: "He knows they can turn on you at any time."

If McCain was no longer a hurdle, some of the tactics and atmospherics Bush had used to make the Arizona senator go away might be a problem. The independents and ticket-splitters who had gone for McCain fit the profile of the kind of voters who determine the outcome of national elections. The challenge ahead for Rove was to reposition Bush in a way that made him palatable to these swing voters—McCain voters—who would decide the election in November.

The overt religiosity of the Republican contest—and of Bush himself—was a potential problem. Voters do not mind a deeply religious president, and Bush certainly needed the evangelicals in his corner, but there was something clumsy about the way Bush discussed his faith that left moderates uneasy. An early example came during a debate among the Republican candidates in Iowa on December 13. The moderator, John Bachman, asked them "what political philosopher or thinker" they most identified with. Even in a field that included Alan Keyes and Gary Bauer, two evangelicals who routinely cited God's will as their guide on domestic political policy, Bush's answer was striking. Steve Forbes mentioned John Locke and Thomas Jefferson. Keyes cited *all* the framers of the Constitution. Orrin Hatch answered Abraham Lincoln and Ronald Reagan; McCain named Theodore Roosevelt. When it was Bush's turn, he blurted out, "Christ, because he changed my heart." When Bachman sought to get him to expound on this answer, Bush struggled. "Well, if they don't know, it's going to be hard to explain," Bush said. "When you turn your heart and your life over to Christ, when you accept Christ as the savior, it changes your heart. It changes your life. And that's what happened to me."

Leaving aside the point that Bush's answer wasn't really responsive to the question, it was unimpressive on two other levels. Given a chance to explain Jesus' importance and the significance of his teachings to world history in a secular way, Bush had not done so. But neither had Bush witnessed for Christ as a follower of the faith. His answer was about as illuminating, and about as inclusive, as a phrase popular at the time, *"It's a black thing, you wouldn't understand."*

Rove, too, has displayed a consistent awkwardness in discussing his own beliefs. During the 2000 campaign, *The New York Times Magazine* revealed that Rove himself was not a particularly religious man. The piece quoted one of Rove's Salt Lake City high school debating partners, Mark Dangerfield, now a Phoenix attorney, who recalled that it bothered Rove that "he was raised in a completely nonreligious home." Asked by the *Times* about his friend's observation, Rove replied, "I'm not sure I've ever found faith. Others here—others in the campaign, including George W.— I know how much their faith sustains them. Some of them have a prayer group. I haven't been good enough yet."

It was such a candid disclosure from the man who went on to become the White House's liaison to the Christian Right and GOP-leaning Catholics that in a 2002 interview Rove was asked about it by Alexis Simendinger, who covers the White House for *National Journal*. Rove sought to dismiss the incongruity, first with a disjointed story about his boyhood friend being confused by Rove's efforts to stave off efforts to convert him to Mormonism, and then, a few moments later with a joke. ("I'm an Episcopalian so I'm not allowed to be fervent in my beliefs," he quipped. "We're restrained.") Finally, Rove claimed not to remember the *Times* story. But it made an impression on others. One prominent conservative, an admirer of Rove, described him, not unsympathetically, as a "a nonbeliever among all those evangelicals."

Such awkwardness can be explained, in part, by the intricate dance every Republican candidate for national office has been forced to learn since the time of Ronald Reagan. On the one hand, the GOP needs evangelical support to compete successfully. On the other hand, Democrats—and the media—are quick to label as extremist any Republican who panders too overtly. The steps of this dance require the Republican to pay homage to religious conservatives such as Jerry Falwell and Pat Robertson, while having to duck when confronted with some of the good preachers' nuttier utterances. A corollary is the soft-shoe Democrats perform around African-American activists like Jesse Jackson and Al Sharpton, courting their followers while pretending not to notice the leaders' more incendiary pronouncements.

But with the battle for the nomination grinding along successfully, the need to keep the conservatives on board while nudging the candidate back toward the center was very much on Rove's agenda

as the 2000 Republican National Convention in Philadelphia
approached. In the minds of Bush aides, transforming Bush back
into a moderate-sounding Republican was an exercise in maintain-
ing quality control over his rhetoric rather than tweaking the candidate's actual policy positions. Rove was convinced that Bush's
policy prescriptions, particularly on taxes, would do fine with the
electorate, even though they were not popular with the press. But
this would hold true only as long as voters didn't think of Bush and
the Republican Party as harshly conservative. Such a perception
had been fostered in 1992 about Bush's father, when his handlers
lost control of the convention, held that year in Houston. Reagan
had given a captivating address—his convention swan song, as it
happened—but the Gipper had been pushed past prime time by a
Patrick Buchanan speech, the message of which was anything but
inclusive. Coupled with uncompromising speeches by Pat Robertson, who had also challenged Bush senior in the GOP primaries,
and by Marilyn Quayle, of all people, the story line that emerged
from the 1992 convention was that the Republicans were angry,
small-minded and exclusive. Conservatives complained that this
was a case of many reporters seeing what they expected to see—and
revealing their own bias in the process. If anything, they said, it was
the 1992 Democratic National Convention in New York City that
demonstrated intolerance—and did so on the same issue, abortion,
if in another direction. Pennsylvania's Democratic governor, Robert
Casey, was not allowed to address the Democratic convention
because he espoused right-to-life views on abortion.

The Democrats in 1992 had also given a prominent prime-time
slot to two speakers—Elizabeth Glaser, the wife of the actor Paul
Michael Glaser, and Bob Hattoy, a Sierra Club official—both of

whom were HIV-positive. In their speeches, Hattoy and Glaser sought to politicize the issue by issuing harsh denunciations of Republicans. Glaser, who contracted the disease from a blood transfusion in 1981 and passed it along to her children before it even had a name, inexplicably blamed the Reagan administration for her plight. Hattoy's language was even more extreme. "If George Bush wins again we're all at risk," he said. "It's that simple. It's that serious. It's that terrible." (By contrast, the Republican convention in Houston would feature a conciliatory prime-time speech by AIDS sufferer Mary Fisher, who worked in the Ford administration and was the daughter of a wealthy GOP donor. "The AIDS virus is not a political creature," Fisher said. "It does not care whether you are Democrat or Republican. It does not ask whether you are black or white, male or female, gay or straight, young or old.")

Bush family loyalists had never forgotten the Democrats' harsh language. Nor had they forgotten what they perceived as the media's double standard. To Rove and the other Republicans preparing for Philadelphia there were two lessons of 1992. The first was that the reporters, most of whom were liberal, could not be counted on to cover the conventions fairly. The second, flowing directly from the first, was that you couldn't lose control of the gavel for even a moment. "Ours will be a different kind of convention because we have a different kind of Republican running for President," vowed Andrew H. Card Jr., the GOP convention's general co-chairman. In truth what the Republicans had was a new determination to control things tightly, and a heightened appreciation for the purely symbolic nature of modern political conventions. With the media waiting to pounce on the Republicans for any sign of small-mindedness, intolerance or generally Neanderthal attitudes, the convention speakers had to have perfect pitch. The right demographics would help, too. And so a convention lineup was prepared that included not only Colin Powell, Condoleezza Rice, and Bush's own handsome young Hispanic nephew, George P. Bush, but also Erik Weihenmayer, a blind mountain climber who led the convention in the Pledge of Allegiance, California Assemblyman Abel Malonado, whose father was an immigrant farm worker (and who addressed the convention in Spanish), and Nancy Goodman Brinker, founder of the Susan G. Komen Breast Cancer Foundation. The theme of the first night, "Opportunity with a Purpose: Leave No Child Behind," gave the convention the feel of a Democratic convention opening night.

If movement conservatives found the tone of the Philadelphia convention disconcerting, most kept their own counsel. One of those who didn't was Pat Robertson, head of the Christian Coalition. "It's prepackaged," he complained. "It's slick. It's homogenized. It's pabulum."

Coming from one of those who the Bush crowd believed had sabotaged Big George in 1992, this criticism didn't cut much ice. But Robertson wasn't alone. Conservative author John O'Sullivan groused about the direction the Bush crowd was taking the Republican Party—he mentioned Rove by name—in an essay in *National Review*. "Is this a Republican convention or the annual dinner of the Bilingual Friends of Feminism?" O'Sullivan wrote in the voice of a perplexed (but mythical) GOP delegate in Philadelphia. "Frankly, I've had it up to my keister with tostadas and I'm beginning to wonder if the Bush people aren't going overboard with all this inclusiveness. Since when does being inclusive mean excluding

Republicans? Or conservatives? Or white males? Or all three combined?" Fred Barnes, another prominent conservative writer, writing in another conservative magazine, *The Weekly Standard*, also lamented how the Bush Republicans had tossed some cherished conservative ideas overboard. Barnes homed in on term limits, and also seemed to attribute this apostasy to Rove, who had told him, "Term limits is not our fight." "So term limits simply vanished as a GOP issue," Barnes added, "and with scarcely a peep of dissent."

Rove also dismissed the old GOP ways as an "old paradigm" and a timeworn "Southern strategy" that would never work again. "People are more attracted today by a positive agenda than by wedge issues," he said in the days leading up to the convention. "If you have knocked down the Berlin Wall and the Evil Empire has disappeared, it makes it a little bit difficult to run on a platform of 1956 or 1960." Rove was saying that in the new world of the twenty-first century, the GOP needed to soften its face to continue to compete in national elections. What is interesting about this in hindsight is how little thought even the Bush brain trust gave to George W. Bush as a future wartime leader. Colin Powell, a warrior by training, was offered up to the convention—but not as a soldier. His was the face and the voice of a moderate African-American Republican whose own stated concerns were primarily racial equity, education, and inclusion.

"In pursuing educational reform as well as in all other parts of his agenda for Texas, Governor Bush has reached out to all Texans—white, black, Latino, Asian, Native American," Powell told the convention in his role as the first-night headliner. "He has been successful in bringing more and more minorities into the tent by responding to their deepest needs. Some call it 'compassionate conservatism.' To me, it's just caring about people. I believe he can do the same thing as president. I am convinced he will bring to the White House that same passion for inclusion. I know that he can help bridge our racial divides—I know that. Recently Governor Bush addressed the annual meeting of the NAACP. He spoke to the delegates about his plans for housing and health and educational programs to help all Americans. He also spoke the truth to the delegates when he said that the party of Lincoln has not always carried the mantle of Lincoln. I talked with him again today, and I know that, with all his heart, Governor Bush welcomes the challenge. He wants the Republican Party to wear that mantle again."

Two years later, in his book *Bush at War*, Bob Woodward would expose some of the nerves that Powell touched in the Bush political team, even with Rove, in the campaign. "After Bush won the 2000 Republican presidential nomination, Powell signed on to help, but Karl Rove found that the campaign had to move heaven and earth to get him to appear at an event with Bush. Nearly every other important Republican fell in line, not Powell," Woodward wrote. "His people always wanted to know who else would be at an event, what would be said, who the audience was, what the political purpose. All this seemed designed to determine the political fallout—on Powell, not Bush. Rove detected a subtle, subversive tendency, as if Powell were protecting his centrist credentials and his own political future at Bush's expense." But regardless of Rove's feelings, when Bush needed him the most—at the 2000 convention—Powell was there.

McCain, too, came through for Bush—and then some. Putting aside any lingering bitterness, McCain labored on his speech, televised in prime time on the second night of the convention, even to the point of practicing it. In so doing, McCain showed that, like Powell, the military ethos of lining up behind the ranking officer (even if you have private doubts) dies hard. "I say to all Americans, Republican, Democrat or Independent, if you believe America deserves leaders with a purpose more ennobling than expediency and opportunism, then vote for Governor Bush," declared the old Naval officer. "If you believe patriotism is more than a sound-bite and public service should be more than a photo-op, then vote for Governor Bush. . . . He wants to give you back a government that serves all the people, no matter the circumstances of their birth. And he wants to lead a Republican Party that is as big as the country we serve."

In his own acceptance speech, Bush filled out the themes of inclusiveness and decency with a couple more. He promised to bring leadership and bipartisanship to Washington, making it plain that he believed Bill Clinton and Al Gore had provided neither. In so doing, Bush sought to distance himself from both Clinton's tawdry behavior and the punitive partisanship of the Republicans in Congress who tried to make him pay for it.

"I have no stake in the bitter arguments of the last few years," Bush told the nation. "I want to change the tone of Washington to one of civility and respect. This administration had its moment. They had their chance. They have not led. We will."

Bush emerged from the convention ahead in the polls and with the GOP's Reagan-era coalition intact. His selection of Dick Cheney as his running mate was the last piece in the puzzle. This choice, the first most Americans outside of Texas had seen Bush make, was contrasted starkly to his father's pick of Dan Quayle, a too-cute-by-half gambit designed to bridge generation and gender gaps. In choosing Cheney, a former Secretary of Defense, White House chief of staff and Wyoming congressman, George W. Bush was clearly picking someone he thought could help him govern. And although Cheney had compiled a remarkably conservative record in Congress, he was seen in Washington as someone who wasn't overly ideological by nature and whose unpretentiousness bridged all strains of conservatism, even those on the religious right with whom he'd never been particularly close.

And so, as they left Philadelphia, Team Bush had all the elements in place. Rove and Card's success in averting a fight over the GOP abortion plank (it stayed in the Republican platform, but accompanied by vague language about Republicans being a diverse lot) kept religious conservatives happy. Cheney's presence on the ticket, as well as Bush's emphasis on tax cuts, kept economic conservatives happy. McCain had neutralized the independents as best he could, and Powell and Rice and all the diverse faces kept the reporters happy—or as happy as they could be with Republicans. Team Bush was also playing the expectation game right. Mark McKinnon was telling reporters that the race was bound to tighten up and would probably be a dead heat by Labor Day. Rove, who hoped that Bush could sustain his five-to-seven-point lead in the polls right though Election Day, believed McKinnon was using good strategy in lowering expectations, but McKinnon was saying the same thing in private to friends. (McKinnon turned out to be right.)

The Bush camp was also attempting to diminish expectations for Bush's performance in the upcoming debates with Gore. This is Politics 101, but somehow it eluded Gore's advisers, who began early in the year smugly predicting that Gore would wipe the floor with Bush when they debated. This played into the Democrats'

Bush-as-moron theme, but it wasn't very savvy. By the time the debates rolled around, all Bush had to do was avoid drooling on himself and he'd have held his own. Rove, playing it by the book, told reporters in August with a straight face: "Our debate strategy can be summed up in one word—survive. We hope to survive Governor Bush's necessary appearance in debates against the world's most preeminent debater." Rove's sarcasm was detectable, but it wasn't aimed at his own guy—or even at Gore—but instead at the Gore team, which had inexplicably raised expectations of their candidate to unattainable levels. In a larger way, however, Rove was playing it straight. The Bush strategy for winning the presidency did not hinge on the debates. Rove and the others knew Bush could pull his weight—they'd seen him do it against Ann Richards—and they figured the three debates would be a wash. Their real strategy for winning the presidency contemplated waging war on two different fronts, one demographic, the other geographic.

Traditionally, Democrats preferred to wage a purely national campaign, appealing to their core constituencies: organized labor, liberals, blacks, feminists, environmentalists. Republicans believed that relying on such a strategy alone makes winning more difficult because it ignores the pronounced geographical differences among Americans. Support for gun control dooms a Democrat in Montana, for example, while in New York, opposition to gun control is considered bizarre. Presidential campaigns, Rove knew, are fifty separate elections, state-by-state, winner-take-all. In the television age, a candidate can't take one position in Missoula and another in Miami, but he can change his emphasis in those two towns. He can also decide which media markets to spend money in—and which states to spend time campaigning in.

As recently as the 1980s, Democrats paid short shrift to this kind of strategic planning. Walter Mondale's aides openly disdained regionalism and Michael Dukakis and his cabal of Bostonians never got outside their own world enough to know how to implement it. When the Democrats did think about regionalism, they thought about it wrong. Harking back to FDR, they dreamed of a ticket that could carry New York and the Deep South at the same time. In today's America, this is a pipe dream. The way for Democrats to win is to secure the two coasts, starting with New York and California, and then carry enough of the heartland to provide an Electoral College victory. A former Carter White House aide named Les Francis tried to sell his party this theory in the mid–1980s, but it wasn't until after the Dukakis defeat in 1988—a campaign Democrats had expected to win—that geography earned its rightful place in the thinking of Democratic Party strategists. A rumpled Massachusetts Democrat named Paul Tully became a complete convert. After the 1988 loss, he went to work for the Democratic National Committee and on his walls were maps, lots of maps, with various colored pins in them that showed how states and counties voted in the past. Tully convinced party chairman Ron Brown that Democrats couldn't win until they started paying attention to these pins, and in 1991 and 1992 both men found a willing listener in Bill Clinton, who didn't build his coalition in his homestate of Arkansas or in Gore's Tennessee (although he carried them both), but on the West Coast and the East Coast and in selected large states of the Midwest.

The challenge for Rove and his team was to reconstitute the Electoral College map in a way that once again favored the GOP. A realistic look at the map in 2000 conceded New York, New England, and much of the eastern seaboard to Gore. California, too, seemed an uphill fight, although Bush made promises to campaign there. Invincible in Texas and the Mountain West, strong all across Dixie—Jeb can hold Florida, they believed—the Bush forces looked to the Midwest, to Michigan, Illinois, Pennsylvania, Missouri, West Virginia, and Ohio. If they were to win, they'd need some of these states. And to do *that*, Rove explained over breakfast with reporters in Philadelphia, Bush would need to hold his own among three sometimes overlapping groups of swing voters: Catholics, Latinos, and those living in the outer suburbs. This is where geographical politics and demographic politics merged. Rove was already working the demographic groups, and had been for some time. At the outset of the 2000 campaign, for example, Rove had put in a call to Deal Hudson, editor of *Crisis* magazine, a Washington-based Catholic monthly that had published several in-depth articles about Catholic voting patterns. Hudson had sent his material to all the campaigns; only Bush's responded. And on Rove's invitation, Hudson brought small groups of Catholic activists to Austin to meet Bush.

Suburban voters, a category so large it defies easy description, were more amorphous. To the Gore campaign it was an article of faith that suburbanites are susceptible to a pitch for sensible growth and environmental protection. The Bushies didn't dispute this view, but they stressed another issue that would give them traction with suburbanites: high taxes. The nation's editorial writers weren't keen on Bush's tax-cutting proposals, but the salience of this issue to the general public could be seen by the fact that after Bush unveiled his $480 billion, ten-year tax cut proposal, both McCain and Gore offered huge—though not *as* huge—proposed tax cuts of their own.

Everywhere he went, Gore dismissed the Bush plan as a "risky tax scheme." On a campaign swing to Washington state, Bush countered with the point that Gore wanted tax cuts, too, but that they were all "targeted" tax cuts, meaning that you got them only "if you do what government wanted." Bush dubbed this, without embarrassment at his evident cribbing, "an iffy tax scheme."

Rove looked at the polling and the electoral map, and pronounced that Bush had an "embarrassment of opportunities" to pick up states that had been in the Democratic column in 1992 and 1996. There were two ways to do this: the first was to focus the resources of the campaign, mostly TV ads and campaign visits by the candidate, to specific geographic hot spots. The second was to target the three demographic groups Rove had mentioned.

Latino outreach had been a priority during the convention itself. In Philadelphia, a steady stream of Hispanic musicians were heard from the stage; one of the most visually appealing rallies of the week was a Spanish-speaking event sponsored by the "Amigos de Bush" at the Philadelphia Museum of Art. Amid signs of "Viva Bush!" and "Un Nuevo Dia," Bush himself addressed the crowd in Spanish and sung along with Latino singer Jon Secada in a Spanglish version of "America the Beautiful." That was the broad brush; an example of a more targeted stroke came in the last week of the campaign in Wisconsin, a state targeted by both campaigns. The *Spanish Times*, a Milwaukee paper that covers the city's growing Latino community, ran a quarter-page ad with a photograph of Bush and this message: "*Cuando Hay Educacion, Hay Oportunidad.*" ("When There Is Education, There Is Opportunity.") The body of the ad, all in Spanish, explained Bush's support for school vouchers, which were opposed by Gore but popular in Milwaukee's inner city neighborhoods.

This kind of on-the-ground campaigning takes organization and money—lots of money—and in the waning days of October 2000, there wasn't much talk of Rove's highfalutin' theories about how the 2000 election was shaping up like the 1896 election with George W. as the William McKinley of his day. No, this was the kind of hand-to-hand political combat that took nerve and brains and, most of all, deep pockets. "We've got more money than God," boasted Republican Party spokesman Bill Pascoe. The trick was to know where to spend it. "We like fighting on their turf," Rove boasted publicly. But the idea wasn't just to take Democratic ground; it was to hold it through November 7. "It's an old infantry expression," said Governor Tom Ridge of Pennsylvania, a Vietnam War veteran. "Once you take ground, you have to keep it."

Both sides believed this, but throughout the autumn, both sides inevitably made miscalculations in how to go about it. Gore grew complacent in West Virginia when polls showed him up by seventeen points. The Democrats pulled their ads off the air to save the money for other places. Sensing that Gore's environmental activism would hurt him in a traditionally Democratic, but economically hard-pressed state, Rove sent Dick Cheney there to promise miners and steel workers unsympathetic to tight environmental regulation that they'd be back at work if they voted Republican in this election. By the time those in Gore's camp realized that they had a problem in West Virginia, the state was lost. Gore also probably gave up on Ohio too early. He never made a visit to the state after the first week of October, and pulled his ads out as well. And yet Bush—

after expending major resources there—carried it by only four percentage points. Conversely, Bush's last-minute swing through California, and his last-minute flurry of expensive television ads, were a
waste of time and money. Bush lost the Golden State by nearly 1.3
million votes.

In any election as close as this one, there will be this kind of sec-
ond-guessing, especially for the candidate who comes up short.
Should Gore have made more use of Clinton in Arkansas? Is there
anything he could have done to help him in his home state? Or to
neutralize Ralph Nader, who cost him New Hampshire? As the
election wound down to its final hours, both sides realized how
close it was going to be.

"This election," Rove predicted with two weeks to go, "is going
to be decided in the last precinct, in the last state, in the last hour, on
the last day."

But where would that precinct be? One place where Gore began
a late, almost stealth, effort was Florida. Bush's polls always had
him ahead in the Sunshine State and his brother was the governor,
so at first the Gore push there was seen as a feint. But when grassroots Democratic efforts in such disparate areas as Orlando,
Tampa, and West Palm Beach began paying off, the Gore campaign
got serious, extending its frantic last-minute get-out-the vote efforts
to the Florida Panhandle and other Republican strongholds. Gore's
running mate, Senator Joseph I. Lieberman of Connecticut, was
practically living in Florida. The polls showed the race tightening.
This was no feint after all. This was a gutsy pincer movement by
Gore. Both sides had the color-coded maps that Paul Tully had
made a staple of modern political campaigning, and both sets of
maps showed that if Florida wasn't in Bush's column it would be

hard for him to get to the magic number, 270, in the Electoral College. By the last week in October, Team Bush had spent $8 million to nail down a state they once considered safe. And they hadn't nailed it down at all. Barnstorming through the state the Thursday before the election, Gore sensed this.

"It's come down to Florida," he said simply.

On Sunday, forty-eight hours before the voting started, Rove predicted publicly that Bush would win the Electoral College with about 320 votes while carrying roughly 50 percent of the vote. Rove dismissed questions about whether Bush could win without Florida as a meaningless "hypothetical"—meaning they *were* going to carry the state. Bush's top political aide was so loosey-goosey that in a hotel in Jacksonville, Rove grabbed a silver coffeepot and imitated a waiter, bringing reporters coffee. The candidate himself was feeling a bit cocky. A day earlier, Bush was asked what he was going to give his wife for her birthday. "New Jersey," he quipped. In this case, the candidate and his "boy genius" were overly optimistic; Bush would not come close to 320 electoral votes, nor would New Jersey be in the Republican column in 2000.

Actually, it was Rove's earlier prophecy about the election coming down to the last precinct that turned out to be correct. And Al Gore was prescient in predicting where that precinct would be. Privately, Rove and the rest of Team Bush was starting to worry about Jeb Bush's state. Jeb was dispatched on a last-minute fly-around on Monday, from the western part of the Panhandle to Miami, with pleas that grew increasingly urgent as the day wore on, to inspire local Republicans to get out the vote.

At a senior citizens recreation hall in Miami, Jeb was the headliner at a Spanish-language get-out-the-vote rally. Florida's governor led the crowd in a chant of "Doble V! Doble V!" On his way out of the hall, Jeb was mobbed by a group of elderly Cuban-American women. "I'm having an out-of-body experience," he exclaimed. "At the end of a campaign, it's like a Fellini movie."

But the campaign wasn't actually going to end the next day. And the out-of-body sensations experienced by Jeb Bush, Karl Rove and everyone else associated with Team Bush were about to get a whole lot weirder.

11

The Last Precinct

On election night all five television networks, based on exit polling from the network polling consortium, Voter News Service, projected Al Gore the winner in Florida. The first to call the race was Fox News, at 7:49 PM. By 8 PM—eleven minutes later—ABC, CBS, NBC, and CNN had followed suit, even though the polling booths in the parts of the Panhandle that operate on Central Standard Time were still open. Rove was stunned and horrified. Stunned because the campaign's own poll watchers had reported back to headquarters that turnout in Florida's Republican areas had been extremely high, a sign things would end well that night. Horrified because Rove knew by then that if his sources were mistaken and the networks' polling consortium was right, the presidency was almost certainly lost.

Rove had had some warning that Election Day 2000 would be a travail. The first wave of exit polls received by the campaign in the early afternoon had shown that Rove's cocky prediction of 320 electoral votes was overly optimistic. If Bush was going to win, it was going to be by the thinnest of margins. More likely, Bush was headed for a loss. Rove felt obligated to share the gloomy early exit polls with the candidate, who was at that moment heading to the gym at the University of Texas with three workout partners.

"I got the smell," Bush later recalled in an interview with Dan Balz of *The Washington Post*. He was talking about the smell of defeat. Rove, Bush told Balz, had been full of "all the cautionary notes" about margins of error and possibilities. But Bush knew right away that what he was hearing "could be trouble." Bush finished exercising, but clammed up on the way back to the mansion. He did not, as was his custom, ask his gym partners to stay for lunch. He prepared his twin daughters, Jenna and Barbara, for the possibility that their dad might be going down to defeat. "The numbers don't look so good now," he told them. "It could be a long night." Later, Bush used the same expression on the way to the Shoreline Grill for dinner with his parents.

In truth, it would be a long thirty-six days. But at Bush campaign headquarters, aides had distributed a schedule for the night's activities, detailed in typical Bush fashion down to the precise time of the governor's victory speech (11:39 PM) and the time celebratory fireworks were to begin (11:51 PM). But as the networks gave Pennsylvania and Michigan—and Florida—to Gore, Bush found himself in no mood to celebrate. Cutting short dinner with his family, he headed back to the mansion.

The networks' predictions galvanized Rove, however, and he rushed to get himself on the air. His message, aimed at Republican-leaning voters in the Panhandle and other swing states, was simple enough: Florida is *not* decided. Get to the polls, quick!

"I would also suggest that Florida has been prematurely called," Rove told the nation in a hookup with NBC anchor Tom Brokaw. "First of all, I thought it was a little bit irresponsible of the networks to call it before the polls closed in the western part of Florida. Florida is split between two time zones, Eastern and Central. You all called it before the polls had closed in the central part of the country. And what is happening is that we're piling up significant numbers of votes in a lot of counties in Florida and the absentee ballots are going to come in very strong for Bush."

In a quick phone call to Bush, Rove was more succinct. "Florida's wrong!" he said flatly. Rove's outrage was genuine. But so was his fear. He suddenly realized that this was going to be *very* close. On the air, trying to retain an outward aura of calm, Rove went through the numbers known so far—174 electoral votes for Bush.

"Tennessee with eleven, West Virginia with five, Arkansas with five, Missouri with eleven, Iowa with seven, Wisconsin with eleven, New Hampshire with four," Rove told Brokaw. "All of these are states in which Governor Bush is doing well. That's fifty-four electoral votes, and then there are a bunch of states in the West: Colorado with eight, Montana with three, Idaho with four, Utah with five, Nevada with four, Arizona with eight. That's another thirty-two electoral votes. That gets you a total of eighty-six. And then we have Oregon with seven. We have Maine with one, Washington state with eleven, and Alaska with three, and we get—we get to 270 plus then some."

But only if Bush carried Florida, an implication Brokaw comprehended immediately.

"Do you think by tomorrow at noon you will have won the state of Florida?" Brokaw asked Rove. "Is that what you're saying?"

It was indeed what Rove was saying, but in truth nobody knew what was going on. He rattled on: "I just got a report from

Broward County where . . . big Democrat stronghold, a third of the
vote is in. Democrats need to win that county by an excess of
150,000 in order to carry the state. We're down by only 10,000 in
Broward County."

Rove wasn't showing off. He was stalling for time.

"We've worked very hard on getting a record number of absentee ballots," he told Brokaw. "In Florida, they keep track of the
absentee ballots in virtually all the major counties by your party
registration. There are 130,000 more Republican absentee ballots
in the state of Florida than Democratic absentee ballots. Plus, we're
going to get a chunk of Democrats and a lot of the 'decline-to-
states,'" Rove said, referring to voters who didn't list a party pref-
erence on their absentee ballot request.

Rove then ran through some vote totals that showed Bush running better than expected. "Let me just give you one example. Here
is a county up near—in between Pensacola and Panama City where
the Republicans hope to come out with a 30,000-vote margin.
We've come out with a 43,000-vote margin. There's a county south
of Jacksonville—Clay County, where the Republicans are—are running 4,000 votes ahead of what we need to do statewide in county
after county. Pinellas County, that we're not expected to win a big
county in the Tampa-St. Pete area. Governor Bush is winning Pinellas County. So we're going to do well in Florida. And I think the call
in Florida was a bit premature."

It was indeed, although in hindsight it is clear that Rove had
been misled by one of the same factors that had tainted Voter News
Service's data: higher-than-expected turnout across the state. In
addition, VNS had data entry errors in Jacksonville and a batch of
bad information from Tampa. Their sample had been compro-

mised. The same thing would happen on election night in 2002, but by then VNS knew that the right response in such a case was just to shut down their projects and let the votes be counted. This time, with the presidency hanging in the balance, they tried to fix the problems—with fateful results.

The truth, which would become plain in the days ahead, was that the vote totals in Florida were simply too close to call by the projection method. When they realized this, VNS pollsters retracted their projection moving Florida back into the undecided column. About 10:00 PM, the networks passed this information onto their viewers— and to the campaigns. But then at 2:16 AM Fox News, relying on a VNS calculation that there were not enough votes outstanding for Gore to be able to make up a 58,000-vote Bush lead, called Florida for the second time—this time for Bush. Once again the others followed suit. And once again VNS was premature.

But the campaigns had no reason to know that. Gore called Bush and made a brief private concession. Rove, with seventy-five raucous campaign workers in town, marched up Congress Avenue in Austin, heading for the plaza where Bush had been scheduled to speak. But as the festive crowd gathered in Austin waiting for Bush to claim the mantle of the presidency, up in Nashville Gore was having second thoughts. As his own motorcade made its way to where loyal Democrats were gathered to hear his public concession speech, Bush's cushion in the Florida election returns kept dwindling. By the time Gore arrived downtown and prepared to address his crowd, it was down to a few hundred votes. Gore's brain trust urged him not to give the speech. One of them, campaign chairman William Daley, apologized to Gore for even having allowed him to make the first call to Bush. Now, Gore made a second.

"Circumstances have changed dramatically since I first called you," Gore told Bush, citing the necessity of a mandatory recount under Florida law. "The state of Florida is too close to call."

"Are you saying what I think you're saying?" Bush asked incredulously. "Let me make sure that I understand. You're calling back to retract that concession?"

"Don't get snippy about it!" Gore replied. He added that as he saw it, Florida—and the election—was still in the balance.

Bush replied that his brother, who was there with him, was certain that Gore had lost Florida.

"I don't think this is something your brother can take care of," Gore replied.

"Do what you have to do," Bush said tersely.

The following morning, the top officials in Team Bush—Cheney, Rove, Hughes, campaign manager Joe Allbaugh, campaign chairman Don Evans and Bush himself—convened at 10:00 AM in Austin to form their battle plans. A team of Gore lawyers, recount experts and campaign hands headed by former Secretary of State Warren Christopher had already descended in Tallahassee. Late getting started, the Bush team wanted to make sure it made the right moves. The first move it agreed on was to counter Gore's ex-Secretary of State with one of their own, James A. Baker III, the Texan who had run Bush's father's 1980 campaign, and had served as White House chief of staff and then Secretary of the Treasury under Reagan. When George H. W. Bush ascended to the presidency, Baker was made Secretary of State.

Rove himself recalls being upbeat. Not because he knew anything about recount law—but because he didn't. He assumed it would take a few days, Bush would win, and it would be a footnote in history. Both the Gore and Bush camps realized that there was a legal as well as a public relations battle to be waged. In Baker, Team Bush had someone who could do both, and when he hit the ground in Tallahassee, Baker wasted no time in pressing the public relations aspect of the case. In asking for "recount after recount," Baker said on November 10, the Gore team was willing to "destroy . . . the traditional process for selecting presidents in this country."

However optimistic he was, Rove was not a lawyer, and he and Hughes (and those other aides whose specialty was political communications) were initially unsure of what their role should be. On the Saturday night after the election, the communications staff got together in Austin to strategize. No one could think of anything to do, and the meeting seemed on the verge of petering out when press secretary Mindy Tucker blurted out, "Okay, we're in a battle here, and five senior people are sitting here sucking each other's toes!" With that Tucker and her staff headed to the airport—and on to Florida.

The battle in Florida was primarily a legal one, taking place in local courtrooms across the state, in the office of Florida Secretary of State Katherine Harris, before the State Supreme Court, and in federal court, but Gore and Bush—two non-lawyers—keenly appreciated the public relations front as well. It was not a legal maneuver when Gore went on national television on November 15 and offered to meet with Bush and open up all the counties in the state to a recount, if Bush wanted. Bush rushed from his ranch to Austin to make a speech of his own. The Bush side was unimpressed by Gore's offer, which was standard recount tactics from the side that was behind: stall, ask for more counts, keep the process going while you look for votes. But Bush was impressed by Gore's political maneuverings. "So long as the Florida Supreme Court was rewriting the law and people were divining intent, we had a battle on our hands," Bush said. "And if he [Gore] wasn't willing to address that, then all the rest of it was PR. That's why I rushed back: PR."

Both sides, intent from the outset on winning the election, were loath to acknowledge the obvious: in a state where 6 million votes had been cast, the results were, statistically speaking, a tie. But the tie had to be broken, and however the case ended up being resolved—either in the courts or in the House of Representatives— the final challenge for the winner would be ensuring that the decision was considered legitimate by enough of the country that he could actually govern. Each side knew this, but there were no guidelines on how to accomplish it. Even Rove's beloved historical analogies were of limited value. They were all improvising as they went along.

As the complicated legal cases grinded through the courts on issues that ranged from the farcical (the difference between a "dimpled" and a "pregnant" chad) and the peculiar (the number of elderly Jewish voters in Palm Beach County who misread their "butterfly" ballots and voted for Patrick Buchanan by mistake) to the truly fundamental (whether Florida's politicized state Supreme Court had violated the due process rights of the voters), the stakes in the public relations battle kept ratcheting upward. One man, Gore or Bush, was going to be a loser. How he conducted himself in this period would help determine whether he would ever be a viable national candidate again. Likewise, one of them would be a winner. His ability to govern effectively after taking the oath of office hinged on acting presidential—before he even knew if he'd ever get to be president. That's why Gore's demeanor on television—outwardly respectful of Bush—was so effective. In addition, the mantra of the Gore team ("Count every vote!") seemed to put the vice president on the high ground. Suddenly, however, an issue arose that shifted the terrain. That issue was the question of late or otherwise technically flawed overseas absentee ballots from American servicemen. Mark Herron, a Democratic lawyer, wrote a memo for the Gore team about how to get these ballots, most of which were presumed to be for Bush, tossed out. If they lacked a postmark, Herron wrote, challenge them.

Here was the kind of issue Rove and the political team had been waiting for. When Gore campaign chairman William Daley had pronounced the "butterfly" ballots indefensible, Rove had already embarrassed the Gore forces by producing a similar butterfly ballot from Cook County, Illinois, Daley's home. But that was a cute, one-news-cycle stunt. The issue of military ballots was more serious, especially to military families, and it subtly undermined Gore's "count all the ballots" theme. Whatever the legitimacy of the Democratic lawyers' position, it seemed to many Americans—including some prominent Democrats—unseemly on its face to advocate the discarding of votes cast by servicemen and women stationed overseas.

Team Bush swung into action. The campaign got in touch with retired Army General H. Norman Schwarzkopf, a Tampa resident and prominent Bush backer, and asked him to weigh in. Schwarzkopf was only too happy to oblige. Calling it "a very sad day in our country" when members of the armed forces had their votes discarded "because of some technicality out of their control, the Desert Storm commander explained that the military's postal system, not the soldiers and sailors, was to blame for the lack of postmarks on some of the ballots. "These men and women do not have the luxury of getting in their cars and going to the post office to mail their ballots," Schwarzkopf explained in a widely quoted statement. "They must depend upon a system that takes their ballots directly from their front-line positions on a circuitous route to the ballot box."

In Austin, Montana Governor Marc Racicot, in town to give Bush some moral support, made his debut as a Bush surrogate—and upped the ante higher. "The vice president's lawyers have gone to war, in my judgment, against the men and women who serve in our armed forces," he said at Bush headquarters. "The man who would be their commander in chief is fighting to take away the votes from the people he could command."

This story line, one of the few in the recount saga that could easily be understood by an increasingly perplexed and impatient public, caught on. The Bush forces on the ground in Florida located the wife of one military man whose ballot had been rejected—and talked her into going on *Good Morning America*. The issue was scheduled to be Topic One on the talk shows on Sunday, November 19, and Gore's team wanted to make it go away. Joe Lieberman was chosen to quell the firestorm. Lieberman did so, but in a way that complicated the legal effort and may have helped put Bush in the White House. Asked about the matter by Tim Russert on *Meet the Press*, Lieberman answered, "If I was there, I would give the benefit of the doubt to ballots coming in from military personnel generally." Lieberman urged Florida's exhausted election officials to "go back and take another look," adding, "Because, again, Al Gore and I don't want to ever be part of anything that would put an extra burden on the military personnel abroad who want to vote."

This was the right political answer, at least in the long run, and

Florida's other leading Democrats immediately sought to distance themselves from the Gore effort to stand on a technicality concerning military absentee ballots. But in real time, it might not have been the right legal answer—and this case was being decided in a legal forum. The reason was that on November 21, in a decision seemingly tailored to help Gore, the all-Democratic Florida Supreme Court had ruled in another context—the context of the "under-voters" that ballots should not be discarded because of the "hyper-technicalities" of Florida election law. Armed with this language and with Lieberman's own admonishment, Republican lawyers applied it to the military absentee ballots, and quickly succeeded in convincing canvassing boards in twelve Florida counties to reopen some of the discarded military ballots. This resulted in a net gain to Bush of some 176 votes. In its book on the Florida recount, *Deadlock: The Inside Story of America's Closest Election*, *The Washington Post* noted that at one point Bush's lead in the recount over Gore was to shrink to 154 votes. Without those sketchy military absentee ballots, Gore might have pulled ahead, forever altering the PR mojo of the great Florida recount.

But raising hell about absentee ballots and some of the irregularities in the vote counting was about the extent of the contribution Rove and the rest of the political and speechwriting team could make during the five incredible weeks of the Florida recount. Allbaugh and Evans had kept a political presence in Tallahassee; Rove and Hughes had held down the fort in Austin. But the case was won in the courts by platoons of lawyers—Florida lawyer Barry Richard and his team that handled the state court litigation in the state courts, Theodore Olson and George Terwilliger before the U.S. Supreme Court, with Jim Baker overseeing the whole effort. But at

10:00 PM on December 12, 2000, the high court, on a 5–4 vote in which five Republican-appointed justices lined up behind Bush, ended the recounting once and for all, giving Bush his victory.

The following day, Rove and Hughes were back in business. Hughes called Bush that morning to discuss his speech. A week earlier, Hughes and Bush had agreed that if the time came to claim victory, the governor should do it from the chamber of the Texas House of Representatives and that he should be introduced by the Democratic Speaker of the House, as a way of signaling that after the rancor of the Florida recount Bush still intended to be the "unifier, not the divider" he had promised to be during the long campaign. Earlier, chief speechwriter Mark Gerson had written a draft of the speech, one that had been extensively reworked by Hughes and Bush, with contributions from Mark McKinnon. But there was something missing. Cognizant now of the unique historic circumstance of Bush's acceptance speech, Hughes turned to Rove, the staff history buff, for some further help.

"This cries out for historic reference," she told him.

"Look at the election of 1800," he replied.

Rove lent Hughes a book on the first bitterly contested presidential election in the nation's history, which was thrown into the House of Representatives after Thomas Jefferson and Aaron Burr had come up tied in the Electoral College. Ultimately, after six days of acrimonious debate, Jefferson was chosen as the nation's third president on the thirty-sixth ballot. "The steady character of our countrymen is a rock to which we may safely moor," Jefferson wrote in a subsequent letter. "Unequivocal in principle, reasonable in manner, we shall be able, I hope to do a great deal of good to the cause of freedom and harmony."

Hughes loved those lines, and incorporated them into Bush's

speech. That night, Bush continued: "Two hundred years have only strengthened the steady character of America. And so, as we begin the work of healing our nation, tonight I call upon that character, respect for each other, respect for our differences, generosity of spirit, and a willingness to work hard and work together to solve any problem." Bush's speech also employed a memorable phrase Abraham Lincoln had used in the context of the Civil War. "Our nation," Bush said that night, "must rise above a house divided."

The Florida recount process revealed a great deal about elective democracy, not all of it reassuring, and one of the most fascinating to students of history is that the traditional concession speech is more than an exercise in good form. It is part of the election process itself; it tells a losing side's supporters when it is time to stand down. It is actually what brings elections to a close. For that reason, as well as media reports that persisted all day long that Gore would "withdraw," but not actually "concede," Team Bush had been keenly interested in Gore's speech, which was scheduled immediately before Bush's. Gore did truly concede, of course, and he did so with class and eloquence. He made a point of referring to Bush as "President-elect Bush," and deliberately chose phrases and cadences that were also evocative of Lincoln—specifically, Lincoln's second inaugural address. "Neither he nor I anticipated this long and difficult road," Gore said of his rival. "Certainly, neither of us wanted it to happen. Yet it came. And now it has ended, resolved as it must be resolved—through the time-honored institutions of our democracy."

Bush, clearly moved by Gore's grace, lauded the vice president at the outset of his speech, and returned to him near the end. "I have something else to ask," Bush said. "I ask you to pray for Vice President Gore and his family."

Rove had sat one row behind Gore's daughter Karenna during

the oral arguments before the Supreme Court on December 11, and it had brought home for him how desperately hard this ordeal was getting to be on the families involved. He certainly knew how badly he had wanted to win himself. Twice, during the crucible of the Florida recount, Rove had taken incremental judicial or bureaucratic decisions in Bush's favor to mean victory. Once, eleven days into it, he'd given high-fives to everyone at headquarters. Another time, Rove had actually given Bush a cigar. But he'd been premature both times, just as he'd jumped the gun with his predictions the weekend for Election Day. But now it was real. They had finally prevailed. Moments before Bush entered the hall in the Texas statehouse, Rove and Hughes spotted each other waiting for the President-elect's arrival. The two loyal aides hugged spontaneously. Later, thinking back to the days after South Carolina, Rove allowed himself a brief moment to crow about what they had accomplished. "March through June, we began the general election while Gore was still figuring out where he was or what he'd begun," Rove recalled.

Years before, when a George W. Bush presidency was a figment of Rove's imagination, and hardly anyone else's, the governor had signed a picture of himself and given it to Rove. "To Karl," read the inscription, "the man with the plan." Now the man and his plan, not to mention his victorious candidate, were heading to the White House.

12

The Crucible of Power

The campaign had been interminable, but when it was finally over, George W. Bush had managed to attain the Oval Office without making many specific promises. This was a good thing, because presidents are expected to keep their pledges. "Politicians are the same all over," Soviet Premier Nikita Khrushchev once said. "They promise to build a bridge, even where there is no river." That may be true in Russia, and it may be true for every other elective office in the United States, but as Rove was aware, it is decidedly not true for the American presidency. In a study of the five presidents elected and party platforms from 1960 to 1984, American University government professor Jeff Fishel charted how, on average, two-thirds of the promises made during the campaign were later kept. Rutgers University professor Gerald Pomper found much the same thing in looking at presidents and party platforms from Harry Truman to Gerald Ford. And in Bill Clinton's first term, Knight-Ridder Newspapers tallied his promises and discovered he was right in the middle of the historic norm—at about 66 percent. Former Clinton aide George Stephanopoulos is remembered, and not fondly, for blurting out to Larry King that his boss "kept the promises he meant to keep." More indicative than Stephanopoulos' unfortunate quote—or Khrushchev's trenchant observation—was the attitude of Clinton domestic policy adviser William Galston, who came to the White House in 1993 and promptly posted on his wall a list of Clinton campaign promises. "I looked at it every morning to make sure I remembered what the President said we ought to be doing there," he said.

Rove wanted to help his boss succeed in office as well, but he wasn't in need of a written bill of particulars to keep track of Bush's campaign promises. There weren't that many of them. It wasn't much of an exaggeration to say that the man with the plan's actual plan wasn't much longer than Rove's White House title, "senior adviser to the president for strategic initiatives." In all those months of disciplined campaigning—of remaining "on-message"—Bush ran primarily on three issues, or more precisely, two major issues and a theme. He promised to cut taxes. He emphasized the need for the federal government to do more to bolster elementary and secondary education. And he said he'd try to restore civility to the political discourse in Washington and, in the process, bring back the art of compromise to the nation's capital. To be sure, he mentioned other issues, including his support for "faith-based" programs to tackle social ills, school vouchers, and the establishment of private investment accounts as part of Social Security.

Still, Rove's agenda for Bush's first year in office was a minimalist one, especially coming after the activism and policy wonk-ism of the Clinton era. Neither Rove nor Bush expressed any grand ideas for "reinventing government," which had been in Vice President Gore's portfolio, or for building bridges to future centuries, or for defining a new world order. During the campaign Bush sounded scarcely interested in foreign policy, and he did not spend the

Christmas holidays following his election to the presidency (as Clinton had) in Hilton Head at the pretentiously named Renaissance Weekend, listening to panelists hash out the fine points of "Global Population Pressures" and "The 21st Century Superpower Sweepstakes." He spent it at his ranch in Crawford.

This is not to say Team Bush was uninterested in governing. Rove immersed himself in the briefing books prepared for him about the beginning of every presidency since John F. Kennedy's. "It's important to strike the right starting note," Rove explained to those around him. "Time is precious."

This was one of the lessons in Rove's briefing books. Another was that glitches arise when presidents try to keep promises they never should have made in the first place, or when they don't prioritize their campaign pledges well. An example of the first mistake is when presidents—and this is a perennial pitfall—vow to cut the federal bureaucracy or, even worse, the White House staff itself. This is nearly always a mistake. They end up either breaking their word, getting rid of essential personnel, or sending the wrong symbolic message. (Andrew Card, the new chief of staff, nearly fell into this trap by suggesting in an interview in the early days of George W. Bush's presidency that he was going to decimate the White House office on AIDS. Card quickly backed down in the face of hostile publicity.) An example of the second danger, putting the president's priorities in the wrong order, had come eight years earlier when President-elect Clinton, a full two months before he was even inaugurated, blurted out that he was planning to open the U.S. military to gays and lesbians. There was nothing inherently wrong with this proposal, which many Americans consider long overdue, and Clinton had first floated the idea during the 1992 campaign. But by

making it his first order of business, Clinton undermined his assur-
ances that he would govern as "a new kind of Democrat." Moreover, gays in the military hardly seemed the most urgent problem
facing the nation. What Clinton should have done, his aides later
conceded, was tackle welfare reform or revamping the nation's
campaign finance laws first.

As it was, however, Clinton's first real legislative fight as president was over the federal budget and taxes, just as Ronald Reagan's
was—and just as George W. Bush's would be. On March 8, less
than seven weeks after Bush took the oath of office, his budget plan
passed the Republican-controlled House on a virtual party-line vote
of 230–198. The package was estimated to cost the U.S. Treasury
some $1.6 trillion over ten years, but such figures are always guess-
work. The bill would cut income tax rates in all brackets until they
were fully phased in by 2006. The top rate would drop from 39.6
percent to 33 percent. The lowest rate was cut from 15 percent to
10 percent. The bill also repealed the estate tax, expanded deduc-
tions for charitable contributions, and increased the tax deduction
for married couples. Predictably, Democrats claimed that a huge
proportion of the tax cuts—43 percent by one estimate—would
flow to the richest 1 or 2 percent of taxpayers. The White House
countered that argument with charts showing that another way of
looking at it was that it was lowest-income taxpayers who would
see their tax bills reduced by the largest percentages. Both sides
were right, and the measure was headed to the Senate, divided
50–50 between Republicans and Democrats and with Vice President Dick Cheney poised to break a tie, if need be—as Gore had
done eight years earlier on Clinton's budget bill that raised the rates
on the highest earners.

It never came to that. On April 6, the Senate passed a compromise $1.25 trillion tax cut, sending the bill into a House-Senate conference committee to forge a compromise. On May 26, that compromise was ironed out—$1.35 billion over ten years. The top rate would fall not to 33 percent, which Bush wanted, but 35 percent. The lowest rate would max out at 12 percent instead of the 10 percent Bush had called for. Nonetheless, it included rebate checks of $300 for a single taxpayer and $600 for a couple, checks that were mailed out starting in late summer. On June 7, a beaming Bush signed the bill in the East Room. It was only the third across-the-board income tax reduction in the past fifty years. The first was proposed by John F. Kennedy, the second by Ronald Reagan. Bush, clearly believing he was in good historic company, invoked Kennedy's and Reagan's names and said, "And now it's happening for the third time—and it's about time!"

It was an undeniable legislative achievement for Bush, although it was hard to tell that from the news coverage. At first, the mainstream media lambasted Bush for ramming his tax cut through the House on a party-line vote. (A failure of the "bipartisanship" Bush had promised, complained the *Los Angeles Times*.) Then, when the bill passed the Senate, the press reversed field, saying that Bush had compromised too much. ("Is this a stinging setback?" asked CBS News. For the answer, the network quoted Senate Democratic Leader Thomas A. Daschle: "If this is a victory for them, then we want more victories just like it.")

Rove and his colleagues in the White House were irritated by the tone of the news coverage. When Gore had broken a tie on the budget deal eight years earlier, the media hadn't accused the White House of committing any grave offenses against bipartisanship.

Besides, fifteen Democratic Senators had voted for Bush's tax cut—wasn't that a sign of compromise? As for the second line of attack, that Bush had been outmaneuvered into giving up too much, on this point Daschle was clearly talking out of his hat. The plain facts were that Bush got his tax cut faster than Reagan (or JFK, for that matter) and that whatever the Democrats might be telling CBS, Bush's tax reduction was three times larger than the one Al Gore had proposed.

What the Bush team didn't realize is that they had stepped on congressional prerogatives. Not by rounding up mostly Republican votes, but by pushing to call the roll so fast, before the entire budget was prepared. Daschle and House Democratic Leader Richard A. Gephardt had warned the White House that such a move would be considered strong-arming Congress. Fellow Texan Charles W. Stenholm, a conservative Democrat, had beamed proudly when Bush gave his well-received address to the Joint Session of Congress on February 27. But that pride had turned to dismay days later when the White House held tightly to its fast track tax-cut strategy. "It just cut the heart out of me," Rep. Stenholm said. "I think the honeymoon is effectively over," added Rep. Robert T. Matsui, a respected California. "They're going to be very right-wing and very partisan." Democrats unfamiliar with Rove's collection of past presidents' First 100 Days briefing books couldn't for the life them figure out what Bush's hurry was. But they knew how little they themselves thought of being stampeded. "I think what happened in the House . . . will be interpreted by many Democrats in the Senate as almost an insult, a slap in the face to a real democratic process," Senator John F. Kerry of Massachusetts said on ABC's *This Week*.

It also didn't help Bush's cause that he had given three separate explanations for why he thought a tax cut was desirable. During the campaign, when federal budget surpluses were projected, Bush said it was matter of simple common sense. It was the people's money, not the government's, and if government was collecting too much it ought to be repatriated back to the taxpayers quickly before Washington figured out how to spend it. After the surpluses disappeared, Bush switched gears, saying tax cuts could spur spending, helping to jump-start the flagging economy. At other times, Bush spoke about tax rates as though moral principles were involved. Paying more than one-third of your income to the federal government, Bush opined, was just plain wrong.

Political observers were also reluctant to give Bush his due on the tax cuts because by the time he signed that bill in the East Room, Republican control of the Senate had vanished with the defection of Vermont Senator James M. Jeffords, who expressed displeasure with the Bush spending priorities. Because Rove's portfolio was politics, among other things, Jeffords' desertion was seen as a failure on his watch. Worse, he hadn't even seen it coming. Nevertheless, Rove was gradually assuming the kind of power in the White House that made him a logical scapegoat when almost anything went wrong. And it wasn't just politics. It was policy, too. Cabinet appointments were vetted through him, judicial nominations crossed his desk, as did the details of a proposed energy bill, administration policy on stem-cell research, steel tariffs, and health care policy. Nearly every speech was shown to Rove before it was delivered. He often suggested changes. The question of who should head the RNC was his bailiwick, as was the ever-constant challenge of mollifying the conservative wing of the Republican Party. When Bush wanted to reward Montana Governor Marc Racicot, a longtime personal friend, for his loyalty and effectiveness during the Florida recount, with the job he wanted—Attorney General—it was Rove to whom the conservatives appealed. Racicot was squishy on abortion and other social issues, they said. John Ashcroft got the job instead. The line separating politics from policy is never clearly delineated in any White House. Rove made no pretense that there was a line. Asked in early 2002 if there was any domestic issue he *didn't* have his hands on, Rove quipped, "Anything involving baseball."

By this time, Rove was well along in remaking his own image. A long time removed from the direct mail specialist whose most obvious talent lay in conceiving of a devastating negative attack, Rove was increasingly seen in Washington as the well-read history buff whose counsel was eagerly sought by the president on almost everything. He was asked in April 2002 in a ninety-minute interview with *National Journal* if he considered himself primarily a policy adviser.

"Well, look, part of my job is to look after the politics of things, but the fact of the matter is, if you make an electoral calculation about everything, it will blow up in your face," he replied. "The best politics is sound policy. The question is: 'Is this in conformity with the President's principles, and will it seek to achieve a goal that he laid out during the campaign?'"

But whatever one called what Rove was doing, it seemed to be working. In Bush's first summer in office, his job approval rating, as measured in the Gallup Poll, hovered in the mid–50s, which is acceptable, but not great. To keep it there—or, better yet, to increase it—Rove needed to keep the legislative victories coming. But just as Team Bush had been blindsided by Jim Jeffords' defection, they also underestimated how much the change of one vote in the Senate would interfere with The Plan. With Senator Daschle, a liberal with presidential fancies of his own, now in charge of the legislative calendar, Bush could suddenly not even get his pet bills, such as his faith-based initiative, to the Senate floor for a vote. Meanwhile, new Judiciary Committee Chairman Patrick Leahy of Vermont was using his control to stall Bush's judicial nominees— and sometimes to publicly eviscerate the reputations of those deemed too conservative.

But even as conservatives were carping that the White House was letting judicial nominees hang out to dry, Rove concluded that fighting too hard on these messy appointment battles was not how he wanted to spend Bush's precious, limited, political capital. Answering Democrats in kind was a trap. They had learned in Austin that keeping the tone of political debate on a civil plane wasn't just good government—it was good politics. In 1994, Ann Richards had derisively referred to Bush as "Shrub," while the challenger always called her "governor."

Once, in his debate with Richards, she made some kind remarks about volunteers who had responded to a natural disaster in Texas. Bush didn't try to one-up her.

"Well spoken, governor," was all he replied.

His civility, however calculated, struck voters as reflective of good manners. And although their private comments about the Democrats could be quite pointed, Rove and Bush resisted being goaded into a public pissing match with Daschle or Leahy.

In fact, while Daschle was first sniping at the tax bill, Bush responded by posing for pictures with Daschle while in South Dakota. "Sometimes we'll agree, sometimes we won't agree, but one thing that Senator Daschle and I have agreed on is to respect each other," Bush said on March 9 while standing beside the Democratic Leader at a community health center in Sioux Falls. "People want civility. We're going to give them civility."

This charm offensive was swell, but with the Democrats running the Senate and Bush's momentum stalled, Rove longed to replicate his successes in Austin, where the typical prescription had been to have Bush push hard rhetorically on an initiative, then let the legislative process work its way. After compromise was reached, Bush could take the credit at a festive bill signing ceremony, often sitting under a big campaign-style banner with some slogan on it reading something like, "Leave No Child Behind."

In Washington, they'd done this on taxes, but now they needed another victory. They needed an education bill.

The "No Child Left Behind Act of 2001"—that was actually its name—passed the House in late May on a vote of 384 to 45, a landslide that included 197 Democrats. This bill, despite its Orwellian title, was a scheduled reauthorization of the 1965 Elementary and Secondary Education Act. The text of the bill was long and complicated, but the gist was that the Bush administration agreed to spend more money in return for more accountability from states and local school boards. What the administration demanded, ultimately, was annual testing of each school in the country—and a series of sanctions for schools that didn't get better. The vote tally was so lopsided because each side had given something. Bush had thrown in the towel on vouchers before the negotiating even got serious, a gesture that showed good faith. His reward was the defeat of a liberal amendment to kill the testing requirements. This compromise had the blessing of Democratic Representative George Miller, a hulking

California liberal with a big laugh, big ideas about what government could accomplish—and a desire to get things done. One of the House's four remaining "Watergate babies" from the huge Democratic class of 1974, Miller had campaigned in 2000 for Bill Bradley, not Gore, because he was tired of "incrementalism" in Washington. Miller's passion has become education policy—and he's willing to buck even the teacher's union to get more federal money into schools and some genuine education standards. Bush promptly dubbed Miller "Big George," the same name the Bush family employed to delineate Bush's father from George W. Bush, who as a boy, was called "Georgie." More to the point, Bush had found in George Miller someone he could work with. The bill they ultimately fashioned—and the process that produced it—satisfied the White House and impressed liberals. "There have been extensive bipartisan negotiations on the education bill, there's no doubt about that, and they have been real," proclaimed Ralph Neas, president of People for the American Way. But if the rapport between "Georgie" and "Big George" was impressive, it was nothing compared to the unusual alliance the president formed with Senator Edward M. Kennedy.

Republican candidates—and Republican political operatives such as Karl Rove—spend so much of their time bashing Ted Kennedy on their way up the ladder that they are invariably and pleasantly surprised when they finally meet the man. He is personable and earthy; he has the Kennedy charisma and is disarmingly candid and straightforward in his closed-door legislative negotiations. Bush laid the groundwork even before his inauguration by calling Kennedy. And in his first week in office, he invited Kennedy and much of his clan to the White House for a screening of the movie *Thirteen Days.* (The invitees included Representative Patrick Kennedy, who had said during the 2000 South Carolina primary that the visit to Bob Jones University proved Bush was a "wing nut." About his invitation to eat hot dogs and hamburgers in the White House theater, Patrick Kennedy remarked, "I thought it was very gracious of him to invite me.") After Kennedy and Bush found common ground on the education bill, Bush literally traveled around the country singing Kennedy's praises. "I told the folks at the coffee shop in Crawford, Texas, that Ted Kennedy was all right," Bush said at one joint appearance. "They nearly fell out. But he is. I've come to admire him. He's a smart, capable senator. You want him on your side, I can tell you that."

If this was vaguely patronizing—certainly not everyone in Crawford considers Kennedy a pariah—the senator went along. In the scheme of things, the relationship with Bush helped him, too: Beneath the banter was the tacit implication that even for a Republican president, liberal Ted Kennedy remains the go-to guy in the Senate's Democratic caucus. Kennedy walked the walk as well. He personally talked liberal senators out of their misgivings, pointing out to them all they'd gotten from the White House by way of compromise. On June 14, with Kennedy personally sheep-dogging it, the No Child Left Behind Act passed the Senate ninety-one to eight.

"I think the president deserves credit," Daschle said after the vote. "He has been resolute in his effort to find that middle ground on this bill, and I want to compliment him for his willingness to do that. . . . I think this is good for schools."

There was the little matter of spending levels for the educational provisions in the bill, never fully resolved. The White House was envisioning that the new school plan would cost about $19 billion in the coming year. The House version called for $24 billion. The Kennedy version was a lot more—$41.8 billion—but back then everybody told themselves: that's what House-Senate conferences were for. Eventually, this disagreement over funding levels would become bitter and would undo much of the goodwill formed between the White House and the liberals on Capitol Hill. But as Bush's first summer as president was coming to a close, Karl Rove's plan for the first year was proceeding apace. The tax bill was law, the education bill was in conference, and Bush's civility campaign was attaining tangible results.

Rove was pleased as pie, although there is always an Eeyore or two in the crowd. Bush had inherited an under-performing economy, and it wasn't getting any better. In peacetime, a president's job approval rating typically rises and falls with the state of the economy. On August 31, 2001, the unemployment figures released by the government showed the jobless rate had risen to 4.9 percent. The following Tuesday, September 4, at the Metropolitan Club in Washington, about a dozen Republican eminences had met for a private dinner with Rove, White House budget director Mitchell E. Daniels Jr. and Nicholas Calio, the White House's liaison to Capitol Hill. These Republicans, who included former White House chief of staff Kenneth M. Duberstein, GOP pollster Linda DiVall, conservative activist David Keene, and a former party chairman Haley Barbour, had no specific agenda. But as the dinner progressed, several of them voiced concern that the administration wasn't acting decisively enough on the economy. They wanted Bush to do something—exactly what was not a matter of consensus—and suggested that Republican candidates in 2002 would be at peril if the economy were still sluggish and Bush was perceived as being passive about it.

Rove mostly listened at that dinner. A few of these Republicans were his friends or allies from past campaigns, but he thought they were being a little panicky. "A lot of people in Washington are trying to dismiss the success of this president by raising the bar higher on the next thing down the pike," he complained a few days later. Besides, Rove already had big plans. He was planning on getting active himself in speaking at GOP fundraisers. And he was devising ways to get more out of Laura Bush, who as a campaigner and a public speaker was proving to be a huge, and popular, draw. Several such appearances, mostly for female GOP candidates, had already been scheduled for later in the month. Rove also had mapped out ways to keep the focus on the education bill, which seemed stuck in that House-Senate conference committee

The following Tuesday, Laura Bush was scheduled to testify on Capitol Hill on early childhood development. As it happens, she was to appear before Kennedy's Senate committee. Rove himself was heading to Florida for a couple of days with the president, who was scheduled to begin a week of education-related speeches and media events focusing on reading. The first school on the list was Justina Road Elementary School in Jacksonville on Monday, September 10. The second, the following morning, was Emma E. Booker Elementary in Sarasota. And that's where they were when the planes hit.

During the Florida recount, the lawyers had realized that spin and political strategizing might help, but that the real work had to be done by the experts. Rove and Karen Hughes had abided by that judgment; they had done what they could, but it was precious little.

On the surface, war might seem a similar set of circumstances. The war would be won by the generals and the soldiers and the civilians with martial backgrounds, be they Secretary of Defense Donald H. Rumsfeld or "Gary," the CIA station chief who choppered into Afghanistan with $3 million in cash for inducing fickle warlords to side with the United States instead of the Taliban. But it became apparent within hours on September 11, 2001, that communicating with the public is as important a mission as an American commander in chief has during wartime.

The morning of the attacks, Bush and his entourage (which included Rove; Andy Card; Dan Bartlett, who was Hughes' deputy; White House press secretary Ari Fleischer; another press aide named Gordon Johndroe; education adviser Sandy Kress and Representative Dan Miller of Florida) followed the advice of their Secret Service detail instead of their gut instincts. This was a public relations mistake, one of the last Bush would make for months. Air Force One didn't head north toward the White House, but west to Barksdale Air Force Base, in northwestern Louisiana. There, Bush taped a statement, relayed fuzzily by the networks because of technical difficulties. The president's plane took off again, this time for Offutt Air Force Base near Omaha, Nebraska. Once there, the president made the decision to return to Washington. His plane landed at Andrews Air Force Base at 6:34 PM, and he rode in the presidential helicopter, Marine One, back to the White House. At 8:30 PM he addressed the nation from the Oval Office in a five-minute statement that started incongruously. "Good evening," Bush said on a night that was anything but good. But the president picked up steam as he read his remarks from a TelePrompTer. He began to find his stride, which would sustain him for the months ahead. In that brief speech, he touched on all the themes that would animate him in the coming year: He expressed sorrow for the victims and their families, especially the children left without parents; he denounced the perpetrators of the attack as "evil," a word he would employ again and again; he vowed to bring the perpetrators to justice, and, more ominously, vowed to make no distinction between the terrorists "and those who harbor them"; he alluded to his faith by quoting the 23rd Psalm ("Even though I walk through the valley of the shadow of death I fear no evil—for You are with me"); finally, Bush said that the nation had been attacked before, and had always prevailed.

"America has stood down enemies before, and we will do so this time," he said that night. "None of us will ever forget this day. Yet, we go forward to defend freedom and all that is good and just in our world."

Bush deliberately avoided using the phrase "act of war" that night, which he thought the country might not be ready for in those uncertain hours. But he did use it the following day, in a grim-faced comment to the White House "pool" of reporters gathered for photographs as Bush sat down with his national security team. His remarks included the following passage:

> The American people need to know that we're facing a different enemy than we have ever faced. This enemy hides in shadows, and has no regard for human life. This is an enemy who preys on innocent and unsuspecting people, then runs for cover. But it won't be able to run for cover forever. This is an enemy that tries to hide. But it won't be able to hide forever. This is an enemy that thinks its harbors are safe. But they won't be safe forever.

This enemy attacked not just our people, but all freedom-loving people everywhere in the world. The United States of America will use all our resources to conquer this enemy. We will rally the world. We will be patient, we will be focused, and we will be steadfast in our determination.

This battle will take time and resolve. But make no mistake about it: we will win.

For well over a year after the attacks, Rove and other White House advisers insisted that, contrary to what anyone said, Bush did not "grow" in office. They maintained that he was always the steely, substantive fellow on display on September 12. It is unclear why they do this: The evidence is all in the other direction, and it is hardly unflattering to Bush that he rose to the occasion and did so almost immediately. Nor that he had help in doing so, not only from Rumsfeld and Colin Powell, but from Rove, Hughes, Gerson, Bartlett, and others in the White House communications shop.

Long before September 11, Bush had shown he knew how to hire speechwriters, and that he could deliver a written speech. It was a good thing—because Bush Unplugged could certainly be something to behold. During the campaign he had mesmerized the press with such Quayle-like rhetorical flights of fancy as "We won't raise trade terriers," and "We ought to make the pie higher." He once allowed as how "more and more of our imports come from overseas," and riffed that, "Families is where our nation finds shape, where wings take dream." As president he dazzled audiences with made up words such as the redundant, but catchy "misunderestimate" or the descriptive "embetterment," apparently inspired by the co-mingling of "empowerment" and "betterment."

On occasion, the unscripted Bush would just leave his listeners wondering exactly what was taking place inside his head. Consider this exchange with the White House pool on July 2, 2001, at the Jefferson Memorial.

Q. What's the occasion, Mr. President?

BUSH. Wanted to come over. We're looking right out our window every day at the Jefferson. It's a beautiful day. Wanted to come over and begin the beginning of the Fourth of July celebration here at the Jefferson Memorial; it's an opportunity to say hello to some of our fellow Americans.

Q. What does the Fourth mean to you, Mr. President?

BUSH. Well, it's an unimaginable honor to be the President during the Fourth of July of this country. It means what these words say, for starters. The great inalienable rights of our country. We're blessed with such values in America. And I—it's—I'm a proud man to be the nation based upon such wonderful values. I can't tell you what it's like to be in Europe, for example, to be talking about the greatness of America. But the true greatness of America are the people. And it's another reason we're here, is to be able to say hello to some of our fellow Americans who are here to celebrate.

Just eight weeks later, this man would be a wartime commander in chief to a hard-hit nation—and that level of communication wasn't going to cut it. This is where Rove, Bartlett, Gerson, and Hughes really earned their stripes. As the war took shape, Rove slipped from the news; to those who asked, he would say self-effacingly, "I don't do intelligence." It was true, but only as far as it went. Bush's communications team had never been more invaluable. They were not making policy in Afghanistan, but they were helping the president craft every formal utterance he made on the war—as the whole world looked on. After Bush's powerful remarks to the pool on Wednesday, the staff prepared for what all thought would be their toughest challenge. On Friday, September 14, Bush was to give a speech at Washington National Cathedral and then travel to New York, to Ground Zero, to visit with some of the families of the missing.

It started well enough. The speech at National Cathedral was a triumph. "We are here in the middle hour of our grief," the president began with simple eloquence, to an audience that included his father, his predecessor, and the man who nearly beat him in Florida. "So many have suffered so great a loss, and today we express our nation's sorrow. We come before God to pray for the missing and the dead, and for those who love them."

But the National Cathedral speech was much more than a prayer service. Although the setting was a church, it was a martial address intended to rally a nation, and serve notice to the world. "This conflict was begun on the timing and terms of others," Bush said in words that, like the December 2000 victory speech at the Texas statehouse, were inspired by the phrasings of Lincoln. "It will end in a way and at an hour of our choosing. Our purpose as a nation is firm."

The very eloquence of such words presented a potential problem for Bush. If the gap between those speeches and the unscripted Bush were too great—if the rhetorical bumbler of the Jefferson Memorial were to reappear—it would be jarring to the American people. Just hours after he left National Cathedral, Bush was put to the test.

This time Rove couldn't help his onetime pupil. Neither could

Gerson the great wordsmith nor Hughes, who was so close to Bush that she once said that she didn't know where he started and she left off. Bush was on his own. The scene was the World Trade Center pile.

Bush had gone there to look, and make a show of support to the rescue workers at the site. As he passed through the area they shouted to him, "Whatever it takes!" and "Don't let me down!" A familiar chant went up, "USA! USA! USA!" Rove and the other White House aides got goose bumps. It dawned on them that Bush needed to say something back.

"They want to hear him," Nina Bishop, a member of the White House advance staff yelled in the din. She was trying to make herself heard to Rove, who was walking near the president.

"They want to hear their president!"

No provision had been made for Bush to speak. There was no sound system, no stage, nowhere he could even be seen by the rescue crews, let alone heard.

"Can you find a bullhorn?" Rove asked Bishop.

The president climbed atop a burned-out fire truck where he joined a retired New York fireman named Bob Beckwith, one of the volunteers who'd responded to the attack. Beckwith tried to get down, but Bush put his arm around him, motioning him to stay. A bullhorn somehow appeared out of the crowd and was handed up to Bush. The chant of "USA!" began anew.

"Thank you all," Bush began. "I want you all to know . . . "

"CAN'T HEAR YOU!" one of the workers shouted from the crowd.

"I can't go any louder," Bush protested before starting again. "America today is on bended knee in prayer for the people whose lives were lost here . . . "

"I CAN'T HEAR YOU," came another voice from the crowd.

Bush looked briefly taken aback. But then, his arm still around the aging fireman's shoulder, he shouted back through his bullhorn in a scene aired around the world. "I can hear *you*! The rest of the world hears you. And the people who knocked these buildings down will hear all of us soon!"

When asked about Bush's popularity, Bush's success after September 11, Karl Rove himself would invariably point to this moment at Ground Zero, to a moment when Bush, without polls, talking points, any four-point plans, or even so much as a scribbled note, had indeed answered the call in such an evocative, natural way.

Who knew Bush had this in him?

We all did, Rove insisted.

Maybe that's right. If so, then perhaps the true nature of Rove's "genius" was simply this: Way back in their Texas days, he saw it first.

13

The End of Democratic America?

Two months after the terrorist attacks, Americans went to the polls for the first time in the era of the George W. Bush presidency. On that day, November 6, 2001, U.S. troops were in the process of collapsing the Taliban and scattering Al Qaeda to the four winds. With Americans rallying to the flag and their commander in chief, Bush's job approval rating hit 90 percent in the Gallup Poll, a historic high previously reached only by one other president—Bush's father—since Gallup began asking the question in the time of Franklin Delano Roosevelt.

And yet the first test of Bush's coattails in such an environment was a fiasco for the GOP. Three big races were held that day: the governor's races in Virginia and New Jersey and the mayoral race in New York City. Democrats captured the statehouses in Virginia and New Jersey. In New York Michael Bloomberg won while running as a Republican, but Bloomberg had been a registered Democrat who admired Bill Clinton and contributed to Democratic candidates; running as a Republican was a ruse to assure him a place on the general election ballot. Even then, Bloomberg only won because of disarray and racial politicking on the Democratic side and because outgoing, term-limited Mayor Rudolph W. Giuliani had campaigned for him.

Rove was peeved at the performance of the Republican Party apparatus he was supposed to be overseeing. Perhaps New Jersey couldn't be saved—the state had gone for Gore in 2000—but Virginia was another matter. Virginia's governorship had been open because it, alone among the fifty states, allows its governor only one four-year term. But Rove believed he'd taken steps to hold Virginia, which has become a Republican-leaning state in the past two decades, and that others had dropped the ball: namely the state's outgoing governor, James S. Gilmore III. The loss of the Richmond statehouse set in motion changes that would prove significant in 2002.

At the time of the 2001 election, Gilmore was chairman of the Republican National Committee. He had been installed there by Bush, who had befriended the Virginian when both were southern governors. Gilmore was a Bush kind of Republican. He made it his mission to court minority voters and union leaders, and he stressed education as his number one issue. In fact, Gilmore's 1997 campaign slogan, "Education First, Then Cut Taxes," was a kind of precursor to "compassionate conservatism." In his tenure as governor, Gilmore had approached his goal of securing Republican control in the Legislature with a tenacity and a shrewdness that belied his reputation as a technocrat. He appointed seven conservative Democrats to posts in his administration—and then campaigned for Republicans in the special elections to fill their vacant seats in the Legislature. These districts had, over time, become more conservative and Republican candidates won them all. As part of this effort, the decidedly uncharismatic Gilmore imported Republicans

with more sizzle to be the headliners at GOP fundraisers. One of
them was George W. Bush, who appeared at two events. Bush's wife
spoke at a third Virginia fundraiser, his father at a fourth. And even
though Bush was simpatico with Gilmore, all this help didn't come
without strings. With Rove as the go-between, the governor agreed
to move Virginia's 2000 primary to February 29, as a kind of second "firewall" in case South Carolina didn't pan out. Thus was Jim
Gilmore introduced to the fact that doing business with Rove generally carried a price tag.

In the wake of the 2001 election, the relationship between the
two men became stressed past the point where it probably could be
fixed. The White House had counted on Gilmore to keep Virginia in
Republican hands, but he hadn't done it. And in Rove's mind
Gilmore had all but sabotaged that effort by picking a fight over the
budget with the Republican-controlled Legislature in the summer of
2001, thus giving the Democratic candidate, Mark Warner, an
opening to run as someone who would get things done—a
"reformer with results," you could say. Gilmore believed he had no
choice but to fight the good fight on the budget. But in Rove's shop,
the consensus was that Gilmore hadn't kept his eye on the big picture, which was another way of saying he hadn't paid sufficient deference to what was good for the White House. Gilmore's real
transgression was that he actually thought he was in charge at the
RNC. The negotiations over his titles and duties had taken place
between Rove and Gilmore's chief of staff, Boyd Marcus. Originally, Rove offered Gilmore the more ceremonial title of "general
chairman," but Marcus insisted that Gilmore not be a ceremonial
head. Eventually, Gilmore was given the title of chairman, but Rove
installed his own man, Jack Oliver, as deputy chairman. Oliver, a

longtime Bush family loyalist from Missouri, was the finance chairman of the Bush 2000 presidential campaign, and essentially reported to Rove. This didn't sit well with Gilmore, who ordered Oliver not to convene any senior-level RNC meetings unless Gilmore was present.

But after the 2001 election debacle, Gilmore's sensibilities became moot, at least at the White House. He was eased out of the RNC post in favor of Marc Racicot, the man Bush and Rove had originally wanted as Attorney General. Another former governor, and one who was much closer to Bush personally, Racicot had proved his mettle during the Florida recount. His political acumen was respected at the White House; more importantly, his loyalty to Bush was above question.

The installation of Racicot at the RNC meant that the 2002 Republican political team was in place. At the White House, Rove had as his deputies Chris Henick, a fifth-generation Mississippian from Yazoo City whom Rove had imported to the Austin staff in 1994, and Rove's protégé, White House political director Kenneth B. Mehlman, a thirty-four-year-old Baltimore native with a degree from Harvard Law School. Mehlman was known for working fourteen-hour days, broken up only by his penchant for seven-mile runs, which he often undertook with his cell phone plastered to his ear. Both men are intensely loyal to Rove.

Despite the coup at the RNC, Rove still had to share power with two congressional Republicans. They were Representative Thomas M. Davis III, another Virginian, and Senator Bill Frist of Tennessee. Davis headed the Republican Congressional Campaign Committee; Frist chaired the Republican Senatorial Campaign Committee. Davis and Frist are strong-minded men, but the friction between them and Rove was kept to a minimum by the fact that at the top of this political pyramid was a president who enjoyed the near-total loyalty of Republicans on Capitol Hill and a level of fealty among grassroots Republicans that was almost unheard of. As 2002 dawned, Bush's job approval rating remained around 84 percent. Among self-identified Republicans it was 99 percent. These were the kinds of numbers that left pollsters at Gallup searching in their archives for something to compare it to. Liberal pundits were forced to take solace in gallows humor. (In one *New Yorker* cartoon, a generic politician is being given a presentation on the polls by his handlers; the numbers show his approval ratings have literally gone off the charts, going well past 100 percent. The handlers look smugly satisfied, while the skeptical candidate asks if it isn't likely that "the voters are toying with us." It was becoming that kind of year.)

Democrats didn't expect Bush's gravity-defying approval rating to last forever. Neither did Rove, who instructed Ari Fleischer, the White House press secretary, to start lowering expectations. Fleischer did so, telling reporters that the president realized his numbers would inevitably drop by the time the 2002 midterm elections rolled around. What nobody knew for sure was how much they would decline.

And so as the 2002 midterm season began, the RNC was marching in lockstep with the White House, where Rove was in operational control of all things political—and of a number of policy matters perceived to have political ramifications. It was Rove, for instance, who helped steer the administration into implementing steel tariffs aimed at Europe and Japan. Those countries squawked, as did ideologically pure economic conservatives, who complained that the policy seemed mostly motivated to help Bush in key battleground states of Pennsylvania, Ohio, and West Virginia. Rove ignored the criticism. He concentrated his attention on pleasing his sole client, the president of the United States. Rove argued to Bush that on the merits, the steel tariffs were the right policy, and that the Japanese and Europeans subsidized their steel producers in ways that disadvantaged Americans. Rove also weighed in on a long-standing controversy seemingly far out of his area of expertise: the Navy's use of Vieques Island in Puerto Rico as a bombing range. The Navy and pro-military members of Congress defended the use of the site, saying that there simply was nowhere else on the planet that was as suitable for this purpose. But the issue had become toxic in New York. As a way of appealing for support among Puerto Rican activists, liberal Democrats from New York City had taken to going down to Puerto Rico and getting "arrested" in sit-ins over the bombing runs. New York's Republican governor, George Pataki, who had gotten almost 25 percent of the Latino vote in 1998—and who wanted to do even better in 2002—lobbied Rove half a dozen times to make this problem go away. A few days after the last such meeting, the White House announced that use of the base for target practice was to be phased out in 2003, effectively neutralizing it as an issue. Pataki thanked Rove publicly.

But one man cannot have this much influence without ginning up critics. As early as the summer of 2001, *The Washington Post* had published an article raising the propriety of Rove's role in policy making. It suggested that polling, of all things, played a role in Rove's calculations. Even worse, the story questioned whether the Bush White House was all that different from the Clinton White House in this regard. To Republicans, this was an unspeakable comparison. But some of the complaints about Rove came from Republican office-holders. Senator James Inhofe of Oklahoma, incensed over the Vieques decision, angrily predicted that it would "cost American lives." Generally, such critics made it a point to lash out at Rove, not at Bush. "As much as I love George W. Bush, he was ill-advised by political advisers who thought this was a way to win some votes," Inhofe said.

Rove, with similar motivations, also waded into the issue of a proposed new round of amnesty for Mexican immigrants residing in the United States illegally. Bush all but promised Mexican President Vicente Fox that he would take this step. Again, it was Bush's top political adviser who was singled out for criticism by agitated conservatives. In March 2002, Representative Tom Tancredo, a Colorado Republican, lambasted Rove by name. "There are people in the White House—specifically, I think, Karl Rove— . . . who say, 'Look, I don't want to stay up all night, or maybe for a couple of months, after the next election counting ballots, so let's go out and get the Hispanic vote.'"

But making the Republican Party seem hospitable to Latinos and other minorities was clearly part of Rove's brief. Where he was more vulnerable, especially after September 11, was on the question of whether he had his fingerprints on policies over which he had no expertise—and no real business being involved. National security, for example. And international affairs.

Reporters traveling with Bush to Russia, Germany, France, and Italy in late May 2002 were a bit surprised to find Rove along on the manifest. The White House explained that he was there for the Rome portion of the trip. This made some sense. An American President's visit to the Vatican is not a foreign policy meeting in any real sense of the word. It is, practically speaking, a political gesture—

aimed at American Catholics. At the time of Bush's European trip, the Catholic Church in the United States was engulfed by a burgeoning scandal involving sex abuse by priests. Before the president left for Europe, National Security Adviser Condoleezza Rice was asked if Bush would raise this issue in his scheduled meeting with Pope John Paul II. She indicated he would not. "The president's view, of course, is that this is a matter for the Catholic Church, the clergy, Catholics worldwide to resolve," Rice said. It was the answer one would expect from a diplomat. A similar one would have been given in the foreign ministry of a hundred foreign capitals. Except that it was decidedly the wrong answer. Normally, showing this kind of deference to the pope would have made sense. But in the spring of 2002 a sea change in Catholic opinion had taken place in America, and it had happened over the issue of priests and sexual abuse. To avoid mentioning the scandal would have sent the wrong political message, Rove knew. It would have put Bush on the side of the church heirarchy instead of the Catholic laity in a power struggle in which abusive priests and the bishops who protected them were on one side and children and victims' families were on the other. Bush had to bring it up—but delicately—and Rove was there to make sure he did just that.

The pitch was carefully choreographed. Before Bush went to see the pope, with Rove in tow, the president addressed the traveling White House press pool: "I will tell him that I am concerned about the Catholic Church in America, I'm concerned about its standing. And I say that because the Catholic Church is an incredibly important institution in our country." Bush added that he would also tell the pope that he appreciated his "leadership in trying to strengthen the Catholic Church in America."

Apparently, the meeting went well. When the press was allowed in to see the two leaders for a photo opportunity after their meeting, the two men engaged in an easy banter. John Paul asked Bush if he consulted with his father and as the meeting ended, the pope said, "God bless America." As Bush rose to leave, the pope added in words beamed back to the United States, "I hope to be able to meet you again."

In two years, Bush and Rove had come a long way from having to fend off calls from Catholic Voter Alert. But Rove's expansive White House role was attracting increased scrutiny. Just before the European trip, in fact, a warning shot was fired across Rove's bow. It came in the form of a lengthy page-one article in *The New York Times* on May 13. The piece, written by David E. Sanger and Richard L. Berke, related an anecdote in which one of Powell's longtime friends ran into him and said, "Who runs foreign policy, you or Rove?"

It wasn't clear if the exchange was related by Powell himself or by someone loyal to Powell—or even whether it came from inside the administration. But the context of this reference was clear: Rove had given a speech at the RNC winter meeting in Austin on January 18 in which he seemed to be telling GOP candidates how to exploit Bush's handling of the war in Afghanistan to partisan advantage. "We can go to the country on this issue because they trust the Republican Party to do a better job of protecting and strengthening America's military might and thereby protecting America," Rove said.

The Democrats, who had been looking for a chink in the White House armor, were quick to respond. "Nothing short of despicable," said Terence R. McAuliffe, the chairman of the Democratic National Committee. "For Karl Rove to politicize the issue is an affront to the integrity of the entire United States military," he added. House Minority Leader Dick Gephardt chimed in, too. He denounced Rove's comments as "shameful," and called on Bush to repudiate them. "I hope the president will set the record straight," Gephardt said. "This is not a partisan issue."

To be sure, there was some posturing in the Democrats' claims that they were shocked, shocked that politics was taking place inside the White House. But both Bush and Rove had invited just this sort of scrutiny. Less than two weeks before Rove's remarks, Bush had made an appeal to the patriotic, bipartisan instincts of lawmakers. In a January 4 town hall meeting in Ontario, California, that was devoted mostly to Hispanic outreach, the president said, "It's time to take the spirit of unity that has been prevalent when it comes to fighting the war and bring it to Washington, D.C." And Rove himself had asserted in an interview with *The Washington Post* that Bush had told his staff in the aftermath of September 11: "Politics has no role in this. Don't talk to me about politics for awhile."

But Bush did not repudiate Karl Rove. Racicot tried to soften the tone of the Austin speech, saying that in the speech he heard, Rove wasn't saying that the war would help Republicans. Racicot said that what Rove had really meant was that "an unfortunate circumstance" had revealed qualities of Bush's that were already there. For his part, Rove was unrepentant. "I'm not talking about *them*," he said of the Democrats. "Our job is to describe who we are."

Thus by January 2002, a pattern was emerging: Rove and other Republican operatives and office-holders would proceed, as though 2002 was, indeed, an election year, while Bush himself would stay above the partisan fray—a strategy reminiscent of Bush's days as governor of Texas and the run-up to the 2000 Republican primaries. The idea was that the GOP would reap the best of both worlds. Bush's operatives would be working on the ground, just as they would have had the nation been at peace. Bush himself would talk as the leader of a united nation—and talk mostly about the war. In the aftermath of September 11, Americans old enough to remember said the only thing that had ever happened like it was Pearl Harbor. While Rove didn't have personal memories of December 7, 1941, he did go back into his beloved history books to look up the State of the Union Address Franklin D. Roosevelt had delivered a few weeks after America had entered World War II. Some of FDR's most powerful phrasing made it into Bush's State of the Union address on January 29.

Just as Roosevelt had spoken of an "Axis"—fascist Germany, Japan, and Italy—that was "evil," Bush singled out three nations he said constituted an "axis of evil" in our own time: Iran, Iraq, and North Korea. European liberals and a handful of American intellectuals had the bad form to point out that Bush's unholy trio was an unlikely "axis" of anything. Iran and Iraq were mortal enemies, while North Korea's help in building up its nuclear arsenal had come primarily from Pakistan, America's new ally in the war on terrorism, and from China. But if the Bush-Rove historical analogy was inexact, the echoes in the speech of the voices of American presidents were palpable. And it struck a chord with its listeners. Liberal commentator Mark Shields, among the 94 percent of Americans with a positive reaction to the address, called it a "noble speech." Historian Doris Kearns Goodwin said that Bush's "galvanizing words" brought to mind Roosevelt himself. There were other powerful echoes as well. In one passage, Bush evoked Lincoln, Kennedy and his own father, one right after the other.

"After America was attacked, it was as if our entire country looked into a mirror and saw our better selves," Bush said. "We were reminded that we are citizens, with obligations to each other, to our country, and to history. We began to think less of the goods we can accumulate, and more about the good we can do."

The "mirror" imagery recalled Lincoln's 1861 inaugural phrase, "the better angels of our nature." Bush's words about obligations to country paralleled JFK's "Ask not what your country can do for you" from his 1961 inaugural address. Thinking beyond material possessions evoked his own father's challenge to be a point of light, and extended his own theme of "compassionate conservatism." For emotion, Bush turned to the old master, Ronald Reagan. Bush singled out the widow of slain CIA operative Michael Spann in the audience, quoting the conclusion of her eulogy to her fallen husband: "*Semper fi*, my love." Mrs. Spann stood, nodded at Bush and mouthed the words, "Thank you." Reagan, who popularized this device, would have been proud.

Bush did not go so far as to pretend there wasn't a campaign looming over the horizon. He just acted as though it wasn't going to change a thing he said or did—even as the issues he raised were designed to ripen in November. "I'm a proud party man," Bush said on a campaign-style trip to Oregon in January. "But I'm American first, and that's what we ought to be dealing with when it comes to legislation. There are troubling signs that some in the nation's capital want to go back to the old ways. And I don't think we ought to let them do that." He didn't mention scuttled judicial appointments, a stalled homeland security bill, or Democratic efforts to repeal his tax cut. That would come later in the year, when Bush and Cheney took to the road, campaigning for Republicans on themes crafted by Rove.

Cheney was especially active on the hustings. He spoke on behalf of ninety-six candidates, including fifty-seven House members, in races coast to coast. The conservative magazine *National Review* asked, tongue-in-cheek, "Who's representing the U.S. at foreign funerals these days? Cheney has been far too busy boosting Republicans."

The stock speech given by both the president and the vice president rarely varied. Vote for Candidate X, they would proclaim, because he's a good man (or, occasionally, a good woman) who will help Bush cut taxes, pass the administration's energy policy, promote free trade, restrain the deficit, and appoint judges "who respect the Constitution and understand the limits of judicial power." That was the first half of The Speech. The second half was a seamless segue into national security, the status of the war on terrorism and the need to disarm Iraq. Cheney soon had it boiled down nicely into two short sentences: "The President and I look forward to welcoming Adam to the nation's capital come January," Cheney said at an appearance in Kansas City for House candidate Adam Taff. "He'll be vital in helping us meet the key priorities for the nation—in terms of winning the war on terror, strengthening the economy, and defending our homeland."

There is nothing new about a president campaigning on foreign as well as on domestic policy, or about a president incorporating his official duties as chief executive into his campaign duties as the titular head of his political party. In fact, the Rove-led effort was only too willing to borrow pages out of a book of a president they claimed to have contempt for, but whose political instincts they admired enough to imitate. Upon his election in 1992, Bill Clinton promptly held a two-day economic conference in Little Rock with some 329 invitees. In August 2002, Rove put together a similar forum at Baylor University. (The differences reflected the two president's personalities: Clinton's conference went for two days; Bush's for one, a five-hour session mostly devoted to having people give testimonials in favor of Bush's approach.) The message of the conference was then grafted onto Bush's addresses in an ever-escalating campaign and fundraising schedule. At a September 27 event in Denver for a House candidate named Bob Beauprez, Bush explained what he'd gleaned of the economy.

> Here's the page of the textbook which we read: It says, if you have more money in your pocket, it means you're more likely to demand a good or a service. And if you demand a good or a service, in the American system somebody is going to produce the good or a service. And when somebody produces the good or a service, somebody is more likely to find work.
>
> The tax cuts came at the right time in American history. The tax cuts stimulate economic growth. The tax cuts are good for small business creation. Small businesses create 70 percent of the new jobs in America. Most small businesses are not incorporated. Most small businesses are sole proprietorships or limited partnerships, and therefore pay income taxes at the individual rates. And so when you drop the rates, you're encouraging capital creation in the small business sector of America. Those who oppose tax cuts do not understand job creation and what the small business community does for job creation.

Bush emulated Clinton in another area, as well—fundraising. Rove and other White House aides were quick to point out that this president didn't hold fundraising "coffees" in the White House the way Clinton and Gore had done. Nor did they rent out the Lincoln bedroom to the highest bidder. Moreover, the Republicans noted, when he left office Clinton had bequeathed his chief fundraiser, Terry McAuliffe, the chairmanship of the DNC. This was all true enough; in the midterm election cycle, Federal Elections Commission records showed that the Democrats raised some $199.6 million in the soon-to-be banned "soft money" so detested by John McCain. But during the same midterm election cycle, the Republicans, with Bush as their most prolific fundraiser, brought in even more soft money—nearly $221.7 million. Such dollar amounts had been unheard of in non-presidential years. One reason for the upward spike was that McCain had finally gotten his campaign finance bill through the Congress and onto Bush's desk, where Bush signed it, albeit reluctantly. This made the 2002 election cycle the last chance to raise money in huge amounts. A second reason was that both sides knew the stakes to be high. "President Bush needs the Senate, and Democrats see it as the last line of defense," observed Larry Makinson, a senior fellow with the Center for Responsive Politics. "It's an Armageddon scenario whether you're a Democrat or a Republican."

To wage war for this decisive battle, the GOP amassed a lead over Democrats in "hard money"—individual donations of $1,000 or less—that was even greater. Here, too, George W. Bush was the prime drawing card. And in the waning days of the campaign, this money didn't always go to political activities consistent with Bush's theme of being a "uniter, not a divider." The most egregious example may have been in Georgia, where Republican senatorial candidate C. Saxby Chambliss ran television ads against incumbent Democratic Senator Max Cleland that criticized Cleland's lack of support for the administration's version of the homeland security bill. Chambliss' ad ran pictures of Osama bin Laden and Saddam Hussein before fading into a picture of Cleland. Many top Georgia Democrats, led by former President Jimmy Carter, reacted angrily, treating the spot as though it were an attack on Cleland's patriotism, especially given the fact that Cleland had lost both legs and an arm while serving in Vietnam. (Chambliss had avoided service because of a trick knee.) The best that could be said about the spot was that it was unseemly. Chambliss was shamed into withdrawing the likenesses of Arab war criminals from his TV spot, but he kept the rest of it on the air.

It was clear by autumn, the homestretch of the campaign, that Rove, Bush, and the Republican candidates believed that going after the Democratic senators who'd sided with Daschle in slowing up passage of the homeland security bill was a legitimate issue—and it was working. By October it had become a stock part of Bush's campaign speech in swing states. Usually, Bush was more careful than Chambliss, but on one memorable occasion, he wasn't. Bush typically criticized Senate Democrats for being too beholden to special interests to act expeditiously on homeland security legislation. But at a September 23 event in New Jersey, Bush skipped the niceties and said flatly, "The House responded, but the Senate is more interested in special interests in Washington and not interested in the security of the American people."

This remark caused a huge flap in Washington—it was discussed on the floor of the Senate for the better part of a day—in a contretemps made all the more confusing to voters because *The Washington Post* had erroneously reported the remarks as being in the context of Iraq. This was a small break for the Bush team because it muddied the issue and meant that Daschle's original comments of outrage had to be recalibrated slightly. When the dust-up sorted itself out, the White House remained unbowed and unapologetic. In fact, in the waning hours of the campaign, while stumping in Iowa, Bush employed similar language to that he'd used in New Jersey. "But the Senate has a lousy version," the president said of the homeland security legislation. "They're more interested in special interests, which dominate the dialogue in Washington, D.C., than they are in protecting the American people."

These then, were the dual themes worked out by Rove and the rest of the GOP political team. They talked about the economy and they talked about the war, always in the same speech, and if it struck Democrats that they were being hit high and hit low, they had problems of their own, not the least of which is that they were on both sides of Bush's tax cut issue, and they were openly conflicted on Iraq. At the same time, polls showed that a majority of Americans assigned a great deal of credibility to Bush and were thus inclined to give him lots of leeway.

In addition to shaping the president's grand rhetorical themes throughout the year, Rove and his political operatives were also laboring in the political trenches, doing the less glamorous, but essential, work of party politics. These duties included talking some people into running and talking others out of running. It meant deciding some races were winnable—and cutting other people loose. It meant figuring out where the campaign's not-so-secret weapon, Bush himself, could best be used on the campaign trail—and exactly whom he should meet and what he should say when he got there.

Almost nothing was left to chance. By October, Bush's stock speech always covered the same ground: On foreign policy, he stressed his determination to fight the war on terror no matter how long it took and why he believed Saddam Hussein must be disarmed. On domestic policy, he boasted about the education bill, advocated his desire to make the tax cut permanent, and called for bipartisanship in Washington. On this last point, Bush would stress, almost reluctantly, how that translated at this moment in the need to send a few more Republicans to Congress, especially in the Senate where his homeland security bill and his judges were bottled up by Democrats beholden to their party's special interest groups. Bush didn't generally say that these judicial appointments were some of the most conservative jurists ever appointed to the federal bench. And in Maine, where he campaigned beside Senator Susan Collins, a pro-choice moderate, on October 22, Bush simply omitted the riff about judges entirely.

After Minnesota Senator Paul Wellstone, the most liberal Democrat in the Senate, died in a plane crash ten days before the election, Rove argued that Bush still had to visit the state, despite the skittishness of some Republicans. Rove argued that Wellstone's death was not a reason to abandon Republican senatorial candidate Norm Coleman. Rove won that argument, and he then played a role in crafting a speech prefaced by a gracious tribute to Wellstone. Long before that time, however, Rove had help set up the Republicans' eventual win in the Minnesota race by helping to get Coleman into it in the first place. Polling paid for by the Republican Senate Campaign Committee suggested that a centrist Republican could give Wellstone a real run for his seat. The most logical Republican was the moderate Coleman, the mayor of St. Paul and a former Democrat. It fell to Bill Frist to buttonhole Coleman one cold night in Washington outside the Ronald Reagan Building. For an hour, under the light of a street lamp, Frist explained to a skeptical Coleman what the data showed—and how much the national Republican Party would help him. If Frist, a former heart surgeon who many Republicans see as a potential national candidate himself, was the good cop, Rove was the bad cop who had to help clear the GOP field of other ambitious Minnesota Republicans who fancied themselves senatorial material. Rove called these Republicans and encouraged them not to run. When Tom Pawlenty, another strong contender, balked at taking orders from Karl Rove, Pawlenty got a call from Dick Cheney, who urged him to run for governor instead. (He did so, and both Coleman and Pawlenty won on November 5.)

There was plenty of that kind of manipulation out of the top-down Bush-era Republican Party. When Georgia's Republican House delegation seemed to be taking too long to come to a consensus on who would challenge Democratic Senator Max Cleland, whom Rove believed was vulnerable, Frist helped them make up their minds by throwing the RSCC money behind Saxby Chambliss. Frist also interjected himself in the Louisiana senatorial primary, running ads for Suzanne Haik Terrell, a little-known GOP Louisiana officeholder who happens to be friends with the president, even though a sitting Republican congressman was in the race. Frist also joined Rove in making overtures to Elizabeth Dole about entering the North Carolina Senate race. And in the search for a candidate to challenge first-term Senator Jean Carnahan in the all-important state of Missouri, Rove himself put the arm on former Missouri Representative James M. Talent. Moreover, how these candidates conducted themselves was not left to chance. In many cases their ads were written by the Republican Senatorial Campaign Committee. Rove himself was in contact with the campaigns' key operatives, including former Christian Coalition lobbyist Ralph

Reed, a political consultant who advised several southern campaigns. Moreover, he helped steer Scott Howell, a little-known Dallas-based political consultant who'd rarely ventured out of Texas, into the role of producing TV ads for several key senatorial races, including Coleman's, Chambliss's, and Talent's.

There were missteps, of course, the most obvious being when Rove and Bush recruited Los Angeles Mayor Richard Riordan to run against California Governor Gray Davis. Republican polling showed Riordan to be the strongest general election candidate against Davis, an incumbent made vulnerable by his frosty personality and questions about whether he'd crossed ethical lines in his political fundraising. But Rove and Bush were embarrassed by Riordan, an unmanageable and undisciplined candidate who inexplicably ran as a far-left liberal in the Republican primary and finished third. Davis, with his prodigious $68 million war chest, was unimpressed by any of the Republicans, including primary victor Bill Simon Jr. In one of the most candid self-assessments ever uttered in recent American politics, Davis observed wryly that he didn't need Californians to do "cartwheels" of joy on their way to the voting booth. They just had to pull the lever beside his name. They ended up doing just that on November 5 when Davis was re-elected.

There was also a minor discomfiture in early June when a backup computer disc containing a Power Point presentation on the campaign prepared by Rove and Mehlman and delivered to GOP donors was dropped in Lafayette Park by a White House intern. It was discovered by a Democratic aide on Capitol Hill who had no compunction about making it public. Democratic Party officials, still smarting over Rove's red-meat speech to Republicans in Austin, tried to portray the material in a way that made Rove and Mehlman seem sinister: The two operatives boasted of having tens of millions more than Democrats to spend, and listed several Republican candidates as vulnerable whom they were publicly claiming were safe. In truth, most of the stuff in the presentation, delivered to GOP donors at the posh Hay Adams Hotel, was boilerplate political fare. Still, it *was* embarrassing to misplace your own campaign materials. Hardly the stuff of genius.

In private, Democrats were starting to get frustrated that they couldn't lay more of a glove on Rove. In 2001, they'd tried to make an issue of his delay in putting his stock holdings in a blind trust— at a time when he was advising Bush on a host of domestic policies that had an impact on various companies in which Rove was invested. Rove's explanation turned out to be that he offered to sell off his portfolio, then worth some $1.6 million, when he joined the administration, but was told by the White House counsel's office to hold off until they provided him with a formal "certificate of divestiture," a document the overburdened counsel's office didn't produce until June 6. Rove's answer under-whelmed the Democratic members of Congress investigating the matter, but when it was revealed that the delay had *cost* Rove $138,000—his entire first year's salary as a government employee—in a declining stock market, the imbroglio lost its steam.

Democrats were starting to appreciate the kind of adversary they had in Rove. Political consultant Mark McKinnon was now doing business weekly in Washington. He still had a lot of Democratic friends, and over beers in watering holes such as Fran O'Brien's Steakhouse, McKinnon would tell them what they were up against. "He kicked my ass many times," McKinnon liked to say. "I quit politics before joining up with Bush, but I never had any trouble remembering Karl because I've got his license plate number stamped on my forehead because of all the times he steamrolled me in campaigns."

Rove enjoyed hearing that kind of talk, but he also knew he wasn't in Texas anymore, and it could all go south on him with one adverse election cycle. Rove recalled that going into the last week of the 2000 election, he'd been confident enough to horse around with the reporters on the campaign plane and to make predictions about an easy victory. This time, he took the opposite tack. Asked for his predictions, the boy genius expounded the same nerdy, political-junkie answer half a dozen times, from April until November. Something has to give, historically speaking, he'd insist. "I don't know what's going to happen," he said. "Somebody's going to make history, one way or another. It's very rare that a party in power that holds the White House makes gains in this election; on the other hand, it's very rare that a party gains seats in the U.S. House of Representatives four elections in a row, which is the task the Democrats face."

But if Rove was cautious in his public statements, his strategy was daring. At a time when Washington's political wise guys were questioning the wisdom of putting Bush's prestige on the line for marginal candidates such as Norm Coleman and Saxby Chambliss, Rove was pushing the president to be ever bolder. In the last days of the campaign, Bush visited Georgia twice as part of a 10,000-mile, fifteen-state, five-day marathon that seemed out of character for Bush, a notorious homebody. The president went to all the swing states in which Frist and Rove had handpicked Senate challengers: Minnesota, Missouri, North Carolina, Tennessee, South Dakota,

and New Hampshire, where the White House had thrown its support behind John E. Sununu as early as the Republican primary.

Finally, election night arrived. Bush and Rove had been in training for this since 1993. Bush had defeated Ann Richards in 1994,
capturing 53.5 percent of the vote in an election in which he was the
underdog. Two years later, with Rove making strategic decisions
and Bush campaigning hard, Bob Dole carried Texas against Bill
Clinton while Republican candidates swept to victory in one house
of the Legislature while extending their control of the other. That's
what Rove had in mind for 2002. That was part of The Plan. Rove
could look back on all he'd done: taking the spears for inoculating
Bush and the Republican Party on such touchy policy issues as
Vieques and stem-cell research; bruising feelings to take control of
the RNC; haggling with Tom Davis and Bill Frist—and a hundred
state and local officials—to find the best GOP candidates coast to
coast; helping the party raise record sums of money; crafting the
messages that kept the president at stratospheric levels in the polls;
finally, risking the president's political capital by cajoling him to
take to the road in an election in which Bush's name would never
appear on the ballot.

Election night fell on George and Laura Bush's silver wedding
anniversary. Hoping for the best, the president invited Marc Racicot, Tom Davis, Bill Frist, House Speaker Dennis Hastert, Senate
Republican Leader Trent Lott, and their wives for a celebratory dinner in the West Sitting Hall. A television was set up there, and the
crowd eventually included several members of the senior White
House staff. The president himself was in frequent phone contact
with Rove, who had set up a command center in a West Wing office.

Unlike election night two years earlier, the news from the start was positive. Many of the elections were terribly close, but the trends were all in the same direction. By the end of the night, the Republicans had held their own in the gubernatorial races, expanded their margin in the House, and retaken the Senate. Among the winners were Chambliss (who gave all the credit to Bush), Sununu, Talent, Dole, Coleman and Lamar Alexander in Tennessee, a man who'd once served in Bush's father's cabinet. These were the candidates who'd given Bush and Rove the victory that they, and everyone sitting there, craved so much. Lott would be Senate Majority Leader again and would have control over the legislative agenda, Bush's agenda, once again. Hastert would have a larger margin to work in the House. All the men in that room—and one man who wasn't—could take satisfaction in a job well done.

Bush, who had voted in a Crawford, Texas firehouse that morning and then flown to Washington, put in some thirty calls to winning candidates, beginning with his brother Jeb, who was victorious in his Florida gubernatorial reelection campaign. The president was tired. He'd done a lot in the last two weeks of the campaign. But before calling it a night, he walked his dogs, Spot and Barney, on the White House grounds.

It was about 11:45 PM. Then Bush made one more congratulatory call, his last of the night. It was to Karl Christian Rove.

Epilogue

THE VIEW FROM WASHINGTON

The week after the Republicans' victorious 2002 midterm elections, *The Weekly Standard*, a conservative magazine read regularly by Karl Rove, ran a parody on their back page poking fun at how the mainstream—and in their view, liberal—media might view the results. A mock *New York Times* front page carried the news of the election: GOP WINS SENATE; NATION GIRDS FOR BUSH JUDGES, END OF CIVILIZATION.

There was much more of this. The second deck of the headline in the *Standard* included the line, "Experts Surprised at Voters' Stupidity, Selfishness," along with a large photograph of a Klan cross burning. The caption to the photo was hilarious—at least to a conservative audience. It read: "Ideological conservatives gather for a Ku Klux Klan initiation rally in the late 1920s. Their grandchildren now form the Republican Party's activist base. Coverage of GOP intolerance, Page A18."

In real-life, something different took place in the post-election coverage of the George W. Bush-led Republican Party—and of Karl Rove in particular. The media noted that Bush's high job approval rating seemed to be reflective of genuine popularity. Bush was given high marks for his willingness to put himself on the line for Republicans during the campaign. Democrats were cautioned that they continued to underestimate Bush at their own peril. The architect of all this was given his due as well. The actual *New York Times* ran a piece calling Rove "the mastermind" of a "big victory."

In this way Rove learned something about his new town: Washington likes winners.

In 2000, he'd come to the capital victorious, but just barely. The 2000 campaign had been, basically, a draw. Rove's candidate had won while *losing* the popular vote, which didn't sit well with many Americans. And since he was a political consultant, not a lawyer (the venue in which the presidency was ultimately decided), it would be argued that Rove hadn't really won his first national campaign. Moreover, Rove had been predicting a comfortable Bush victory up until a couple of days before the voting took place. So the jury had been out on him. But on November 6, 2002, the verdict came in. On the heels of the report in the *Times*, which said Rove had "emerged as one of the biggest winners in the midterm elections," came a column in *The Washington Post* by David S. Broder that went even further.

Broder charted the similarities between Bush's rise in Texas and his ascension to the national stage: the narrow victory the first time, one achieved without coattails, followed by the midterm election triumph two years later. In Texas, that effort was followed by a landslide Bush reelection campaign that reshaped the state's political landscape in a way favorable to Republicans. Broder raised the question: Could Bush and Rove be in the process of replicating that strategy "step by step" on a national scale?

"History does not automatically repeat itself," he wrote. "But it would be foolish for anyone, including the Democrats, to ignore its lessons."

Even before such reviews started coming in, Rove's assimilation in the nation's capital was a surprisingly easy fit. Here, to his surprise, the thousands of books he owned cut more ice with people than did the fact that he lacked a college degree. Few journalists covering the White House had ever heard of Greg Rampton, and couldn't care less that Rove was once credibly accused of something as Machiavellian as bugging his own office. One reason was that much of the White House press corps had spent the better part of eight years during the previous administration sorting out a list of shady characters, old real estate records, missing billing records, sketchy tax returns, myriad bimbos, and assorted Arkansas hustlers—all of whom had attached themselves to Bill Clinton in a web of petty intrigue that in the end produced a sex scandal few of the reporters wanted to touch and an impeachment trial all of them had to cover. But George W. Bush was the first president since Nixon not to have the specter of a possible special prosecutor hanging over his head. His aides could breathe easier; so could the White House correspondents. Among them, Rove discovered to his delight, there were a few reporters who were as intrigued by presidential history as he was. Some of them didn't roll their eyes when Rove lapsed into a monologue about the transformational nature of William McKinley and the life and times of McKinley's loyal team, including the great but long-forgotten Charles Dawes.

Rove had other reasons to feel good about himself. Bush and the GOP had raised more money than the Democrats, but in five of the open races that gave Republicans the Senate, the Democrat had outspent the Republican candidate. Rove had the satisfaction of knowing that the difference wasn't money. It was Bush. Swing voters who'd been agnostic about him in the 2000 campaign had, in the aftermath of September 11, taken their measure of Rove's boss and decided they liked what they saw. In addition, the discrete list of issues that Rove and the other Republican strategists had stressed— mostly lower taxes and higher national security—had played better with the electorate than the Democrats' attempts to establish subtle gradations in their differences with Bush.

Nor did Rove find much resistance in Washington to his making the transition from political mechanic to policy maven. "It's been done before," Mark McKinnon noted, citing George Stephanopoulos as an example. "Karl's the same way. He's really got a policy heart beneath his political veneer. He knows more about policy than so-called policy wonks." Speaking for many of the capital's hired hands, McKinnon added, "Besides, all policy is political. And good policy *is* good politics."

The personal part of life appeared to be working well for Rove in Washington, too. Unlike his colleague Karen Hughes, who moved back to Austin in the summer of 2002 because her husband and son were unhappy away from their homey Texas environment, Rove and his small family thrived in Washington. He and his wife Darby found a house they liked right away. The 148 boxes of books didn't easily fit, so the Roves imported a carpenter from Texas who lived in their basement while constructing floor-to-ceiling bookcases on all three floors of the home. Even better, their son found a school in Washington even more to his liking than the one he had left behind in Austin. Rove, relating the story more than a year later, got choked up as he described coming to Washington in December 2000, during the transition. Rove had resigned himself to being in the capital without Darby and Andrew, then twelve, until the school year ended in June, but in the meantime he found a school he thought his son would like. When Darby and Andrew came up for Christmas vacation that year, Rove took his son to the school to get a feel for it.

On the way to the airport for the trip home to Texas, the boy was quiet. Rove was worried he hadn't liked it.

Finally, he said, "Dad, I like it there. Those people are nice. Could I go there now?"

This was the best thing Rove could have heard. It turned out that there was room for one more student in the spring semester, and Rove swiftly moved his family north as soon as he could. Despite the breadth of his portfolio and the fact that one friend once said of Rove that for him politics is a twenty-four-hour-a-day conversation, Rove takes at face value Bush's admonition to his staff to get home and see their families after the work day is over. Rove tried to make it a point, especially on Fridays, to get home at a reasonable hour. The family likes a Mexican restaurant named— what else?—Austin Grill.

Perhaps because he considers himself fortunate in his family life, Rove has reached out to other Bush aides whose fortunes have been more mixed. When Mark McKinnon's wife was stricken with breast cancer, Rove was one of the first to call and offer advice.

"It's gonna be tough for Annie, it's gonna be tough for the kids and you've got to be there for them, but it's gonna be tough for you, too, Mark," Rove told him. "There are things you need to know and things you need to do."

McKinnon, the way people do in such circumstances, remembers who called and visited and sent cards—and those who, because they didn't know what to say, stayed away.

"Right in the middle of helping run the free world, he was there for me," McKinnon told a friend later. "I'll never forget him for it. That's the side of Karl Rove that people rarely see."

When Karen Hughes abruptly announced in April 2002 that she was moving back to Austin, it wasn't a life-threatening event, but it certainly caused an upheaval in Washington. Hughes called Rove at his home the night before her surprise announcement. He told her all the right things: that her loss was devastating to Bush, that he himself would miss her, that for the good of Team Bush she'd have to stay in the loop even from Austin.

For all that, Hughes' physical departure from Washington stood to enhance Rove's stature in the White House. The "iron triangle" had started out as Allbaugh, Hughes and Rove. Now, with Hughes gone and Allbaugh running the Federal Emergency Management Agency, only Rove was left in the West Wing with Bush. There were those, perhaps concerned that Rove might get too big a head, who didn't seem to think this development was altogether a good thing. One of those people might have been George W. Bush himself. Somewhere along the line, after they moved to Washington together, Bush began alternating Rove's "Boy Genius" nickname with another, less flattering moniker: "Turd Blossom." It seems fitting enough, given Rove's modest background (a turd blossom is a Texas expression for a flower that grows out of a cowpie), but Rove shrugs in some embarrassment when asked how Bush came up with this.

If there's a back-story, it's probably as simple as the fact that Bush is vigilant about aides who might be forgetting their place. In February 1999, at a time Bush was coyly dodging the Texas press corps about his presidential plans, Rove blurted out to a reporter from *The New York Times* that Bush would be filing papers for an exploratory committee in a matter of weeks. The Austin reporters were understandably miffed. So was Bush, who dressed Rove down by name at a subsequent press conference.

"Maybe Karl Rove should have spoken to me before he talked to the press," the governor said. "It's best that people not put words in my mouth."

In April 2002, Rove was the subject of a lengthy profile in *National Journal*, which put his smiling face on the cover. At the annual White House Correspondents' Association dinner a week later, Bush flatly told one of the article's authors that he didn't like his aides getting star treatment. Cheney, present at the same reception, was asked if he had seen the piece.

"Yes, I did."

What did he think?

"Grossly excessive."

Picking up on these vibes, Rove was hanging out at the rear of the room, near the bar, nursing a diet Coke and exchanging gossip with the political reporters. The 2002 midterm election campaigns were underway. Rove was sounding like he couldn't wait to see how things turned out. And though he was confident that taking the Texas model to a national level would work, he'd learned some lessons along the way as well. This time there were no brash predictions of success. Rove, who liked to tell people that victors get to write the history, had absorbed the corollary lesson as well: hardly anyone cares what a loser has to say. Rove also learned that "principals," which is what officeholders are called in Washington, didn't have a lot of patience for aides who wanted to take public credit for their success—no matter how many nicknames they had.

"If we win, it'll be because of the president and the quality of our candidates and campaigns," Rove said before the 2002 votes were counted. "If we lose, it'll be because of me."

But they didn't lose, and as the media started to pay attention to Rove, he demurred when asked for comparisons to lustrous former presidential advisers. The names ranged from Clintonistas James Carville and George Stephanopoulos to Reaganite Michael Deaver and on into the historic stratosphere, to Eisenhower's Sherman Adams and even to McKinley's Mark Hanna. Rove shook his head when asked about these names. But some of those who have worked in the White House, including those who worked for George W. Bush's father, said they aren't far off.

"All I know," said Marlin Fitzwater, Bush I's press secretary, "is that I wish we'd had somebody who was strategically as good."

But if Washington had embraced Rove for the most egalitarian and non-ideological of reasons—that he's achieved success at what he does—the implied lesson is that you can lose a reputation as fast as you gain one. In other words, if the city likes a winner, Rove had better keep on winning. The 2002 midterms will be only a blip if George W. Bush fails to win his own reelection in 2004. Several years ago, Stephanopoulos, one of those former presidential gurus with whom Rove doesn't want to be compared, put it this way: "Getting reelected is the currency of deciding whether someone is a successful president. If you don't—no matter what your accomplishments are—all that is remembered is that you lost. You're a loser."

George W. Bush did not come north from Texas to be thought of as a loser. Neither did his personal "boy genius." And as soon as the votes were counted in November 2002, the planning began anew for 2004 and the contest that will truly determine the Bush-Rove legacy.

THE VIEW FROM AUSTIN

At a zenith of triumph and power—his moment in history, perhaps—Karl Rove was only fifty-two. He could look forward to two and probably six more years of being the master strategist for the most powerful man on earth. What was next for him, then? The patriarch and wizard of Washington consultants finally making his millions? Chairman of the Republican National Committee? It was hard to see him going back to managing races for the Texas Railroad Commission. As soon as the 2002 votes were counted, all of Washington was lusting for the volume that would reveal how in the world he did it. Texans, who have always taken great pride in their politics, thought they knew. Over twenty-five years, Rove's reconstruction of Texas into a one-party state could be documented candidate by candidate, race by race. He executed his plan with artful, ruthless patience. Checkmate: That chess game was over. And in Texas, he already has taken on an aura of myth.

One can say he was in the right place in the right time. The elder George Bush, a man born to America's political aristocracy, recognized Rove's talent when he was a young man, effectively orphaned, and sent him to Texas where he could grow and put his zeal and inventiveness to use. A future president is about the best mentor and calling card an aspiring politico can have. The winds of change had already begun to blow in Texas politics; Rove hoisted his sails there just in time to catch them.

One can say Rove was a superb talent scout and recruiter of candidates, and that he had the perfect temperament to survive and prosper in a game not too many people have the stomach for. Ed Wendler, a Democratic consultant who met Rove in the early days, said the young man was utterly devoid of emotion, almost shuddering when he said that. "The man's got no soul," Wendler said. Yet Florence Shapiro, the former mayor of a Dallas suburb, Plano, gave *The Boston Globe* a glowing account of Rove's coaching when he took her on as a client in a tough race for the Texas legislature against two Republicans and a veteran Democratic incumbent, "preaching that she should never—not for a single moment—rely on her emotions, tutoring her in the technique of calculating every move."

One can say that Rove knew the game better and played it harder than anyone who tried to oppose him. Rove has a crack team of opposition research specialists whom he calls his "oppo dudes," whose job it is to pore over bankruptcy filings, lawsuits, divorce records, campaign contributions, and any other paper trail that a candidate may have left. They find everything. "His political bible," claimed Tom Pauken, one of his vanquished GOP enemies in Texas, "is *The Prince* by Machiavelli." Of course, that's a compliment, too. Hardball is a term of virile character reference these days, and Rove has proved himself fearless in a desperate fight. He has said that one of his proudest days in politics came in the aftermath of the ugly South Carolina primary in 2000. Rove was invited on *Meet the Press* to engage the fury of McCain's campaign chairman, Warren Rudman, a very smart man and powerful Republican who felt he had been personally maligned by the Bush-Rove tactics.

"I was scared to death," Rove recalled, "but I was determined not to leave a charge unanswered." He went on camera steeled to make himself look Rudman straight in the eye, and he did.

One can say, too, that Rove has been lucky. Alexander P. Gage, a prominent Republican pollster, said skeptically during the presidential campaign, "It didn't take a genius twelve years ago to figure that George W. Bush—son of a president, owner of the Texas Rangers—might have a future in politics if he wanted one. . . . Personal relationships formed early tend to remain intact, and a codependency develops. There's more loyalty in politics than people realize. Is [Rove] the smartest or the best? Who knows? It doesn't matter. He comes from politics, and he thinks about George Bush and politics from the minute he wakes up."

But when Rove bet all his chips on Bush, the opponent was a Democratic incumbent who was considered unbeatable, and even members of the ex-president's family believed the son who had the most potential as a politician lived in Florida. And the magnitude of what Rove accomplished in Texas goes far beyond one candidate with a gift for hitting long balls. At thirty-two Rove was managing the campaign of Bill Clements, the state's first Republican governor since Reconstruction. He took on a conservative Democrat, Phil Gramm, as a client and eased his conversion to the Republicans. (Party-switching did not always go smoothly in Texas—look at John Connally, who went from being a powerful Democratic governor to a floundering Republican presidential candidate.) Gramm served three terms in the U.S. Senate, and when he decided to retire in 2002, Rove's recruit from an obscure judicial bench, John Cornyn, easily defeated Ron Kirk, a former mayor of Dallas and black candidate with vaunted "rock star" qualities, holding the critical seat for the Republicans. Texas' other senator is Kay Bailey Hutchison, who was an unknown if attractive rich lawyer's wife when Rove encouraged her to run for state treasurer in 1990.

With Rove's indefatigable champion, the president, fervent on the campaign trail, the 2002 elections established Rove as the political star of the year. Democrats could moan that some of those pivotal races were close, but in Texas it was a blowout from top to bottom, and except for tightly controlled fundraisers, the president seldom showed his face.

The knight to the rescue in Democratic dreams was supposed to be the Hispanic vote. John Sharp was angered that he had lost the 1998 lieutenant governor's race to Rove's prodigy, Rick Perry. Texas Democrats respected Bush—had learned they damn well better respect him—but they were always deriding Perry as a lightweight. Sharp calculated that if Garry Mauro had either sat out the governor's race or mobilized all the Hispanics who were supposed to like him, Sharp would have won his race—and then become governor when Bush was elected to the presidency.

Might-have-beens.

Instead of running for governor and proving himself in a rematch with Perry, Sharp decided he could win the lieutenant governor's race if a Hispanic was at the top of the ticket. The enigmatic Henry Cisneros once more decided to pass, so the Democratic establishment served up the race to Tony Sanchez, a squat natural gas tycoon and banker from Laredo. Sanchez had broken with Ann Richards and become George W. Bush's third-biggest individual contributor during the nineties, but never mind that—he had the money. With the charismatic Kirk running for the Senate, the Democrats began to hype a "dream team." Many political observers agreed that it was the strongest slate of Democratic candidates since 1982.

Even for Texas, the 2002 governor's race was an exceptionally vicious campaign. Rove could at least laugh behind his hand that he was busy being presidential. Perry put up a TV ad in the final days in which two former DEA agents essentially accused Sanchez of being a murderer. Some Mexican drug dealers had laundered money through Sanchez's bank, and according to the ad, then orchestrated a hit on an American agent in Mexico. Sanchez, for his part, characterized the governor as "by far the most disgusting human being I have ever known." Sanchez spent more than $64 million on the race, to Perry's $25 million, and against the alleged lightweight he barely got 40 percent of the vote—running exactly as strong as the penniless Mauro had run against Bush four years earlier. Kirk was brushed aside by John Cornyn. Karl Rove's recruits were two for two. So much for John Sharp's theory. Texans voting the straight Republican ticket also slapped Sharp down in favor of the rich but not particularly popular land commissioner, David Dewhurst—about the only major Texas Republican who hadn't worked with Rove. Sharp acknowledged afterward that his political career was over.

The Democrats had hoped that some popular mayors might turn out to be their champions. But Kirk didn't even do particularly well on his home turf of Dallas. And Greg Abbott, another stern Rove recruit off the judicial bench, took out Austin's gregarious former mayor Kirk Watson in the attorney general's race. So much for the mayors. The Republican comptroller, Carole Keeton Rylander (another former Democrat) easily defended her position against Marty Akins, a hapless former University of Texas quarterback. Two more for Rove.

The Democrats couldn't seem to wake up from their nightmare. In alliance with pragmatic blacks and Hispanics, the Republicans had redrawn the state's legislative districts in ways that made white Democrats an endangered species, at least in the State Legislature. The result was that Republicans gained a majority in the house, as well as the senate. Out went Speaker of the House Pete Laney, who in 1999 had stood alongside George W. Bush and Bob Bullock when Bush announced his campaign for president. So much for a bipartisan legislature. Banging the Speaker's gavel now would be Tom Craddick, an abrasive right-winger from Midland. The divided Legislature never completed the task of redrawing congressional districts, but now that both houses were in control of one party, the Republicans let it be known that this would be a first order of business, setting the stage for eliminating the remaining Democratic incumbents, veterans like Chet Edwards, Martin Frost, and Lloyd Doggett, Phil Gramm's victim in the 1984 Senate race. It was just as Bullock had said when he thought Rove had turned the FBI loose on him: "They're out to get us all."

Rove was everywhere in Texas, only he wasn't—the president and the national party needed his focus on other states, where there were actually some contests. The Democratic Party held all the power in state government when Rove arrived in Texas. Now it was like a trailer park in the path of a tornado. There was nothing but debris.

At times it seemed that Rove could still reach out from Washington to punish a Republican who stepped out of line. When Bush became president and Lieutenant Governor Rick Perry became governor, members of the Senate elevated their colleague Bill Ratliff to the vacated lieutenant governor's office. Ratliff, an East Texan with a reputation for integrity and independence, decided he couldn't go along with a radical and punitive redistricting plan drawn up by the most partisan members of his party. As one of four Republicans on the five-member panel that would make the final redistricting decision, he cast a futile but principled vote against the plan. When Ratliff prepared to run for a full term as lieutenant governor in 2002, he suddenly found himself facing an opponent with proven fundraising ability: Greg Abbott, a Rove protégé on the Texas Supreme Court and an unlikely candidate for Ratliff's job because he has spent his entire career in a courtroom. Ratliff decided against a divisive and expensive primary fight and returned to his Senate seat. Abbott moved on to run for attorney general, paving the way for the election of millionaire David Dewhurst—a Republican politician so feckless that the Senate can now be run by a cabal of conservative Republicans. Again the checkmate.

In policy realms, Texas still had a host of problems. Among them, the Bush team had pushed through a tax cut even as the state's high-tech boom suddenly went bust. The Republicans—with not too many Democrats around to blame, if they couldn't do it— were going to have to figure out how to govern with a budgetary shortfall ranging in estimates from $5 billion to $12 billion.

One thing they could count on was help from the master putting spin and gloss on the message. Perhaps that was Rove's most defining talent. It was one thing to keep a candidate for governor on message, and quite another to instill that kind of discipline in a presidential administration, but somehow Rove managed it with an entire party, all over the country. The morning after their great victory in 2002, the Republicans sounded like they were all reading the same prepared text, where Democrats would have been beating their chests and grabbing at microphones.

Bill Cryer, Ann Richards' press secretary, ran into Rove in 2002 in a Washington airport. Rove was with his son, and he was no longer the puckish man Cryer had worked and laughed with in the Bill Clements campaign. "I found him much changed," Cryer said quietly. The day of the attacks on the World Trade Center and the Pentagon, Rove had been in Florida with the president on a political swing; suddenly life changed, and they were zooming around the continent with fighter cover just off the wings of Air Force One. It was a long way from Texas politics. Rove couldn't help but take on some maturity and gravitas.

Where will Rove go when the Bush presidency has run its course and heard its last hurrah? His friends think there's a good chance he'll come back to Texas. He and Darby bought a little bed-and-breakfast on the Guadalupe River, out west of San Antonio. Perhaps he'll become a quiet hotel owner and spend time writing about how he and a few friends changed the history of a nation. The irony is that most people won't recognize him when he goes to town to get the dry cleaning.

The house is in the prettiest part of the state. Amid hills bluish green in the distance with live oak and juniper, the clear river runs fast and cold past banks lined with cypresses. It's the Hill Country that gave the nation Lyndon Johnson, only it's a little south of his range, and a far different place politically. It was settled in part by people who opposed Texas' secession from the Union. Many Texans hoisted black flags of outrage and grief the day Abraham Lincoln was elected president, but he was popular around the communities that grew into Kerrville and Hunt. The locale suits Rove well: In presidential elections it has never voted for the Democrats. Not even Franklin D. Roosevelt. Not even LBJ. Karl Rove is going to live in one of the few parts of Texas that was Republican even before he got there.

Sources and Acknowledgments

Our colleague John Ratliff's patient and skilled work as a researcher, interviewer, and copy editor was indispensable in the completion of this book. The chapter on South Carolina is largely his work. Elizabeth Esfahani's skillful research got us off to a fast start. PublicAffairs editors Lisa Kaufman, Paul Golob, and David Patterson have many hours of hard work invested in these pages. As does publisher Peter Osnos.

Working under extraordinary time constraints, we could not have completed our Texas reporting without relying on the diligent work of journalists at *The Austin-American Statesman*, *The Austin Chronicle*, *The Boston Globe*, *The Dallas Morning News*, *The Dallas Observer*, *The Houston Chronicle*, *Texas Monthly*, and *The Texas Observer*.

Profiles or long features including Miriam Rozen's exceptional Karl Rove profile in *The Dallas Observer*, Robert Bryce's early work in *The Texas Observer*, and the work of Paul Burka and Skip Hollandsworth in *Texas Monthly*, Melinda Henneberger in *The New York Times Magazine*, and David Shribman in *The Boston Globe* were particularly useful. The reporting of Sam Attlesey and

Wayne Slater in *The Dallas Morning News* was extremely helpful. As was the work of Robert Bryce in *The Austin Chronicle* and Frank Bruni in *The New York Times*. The reporting of Richard Fisk and Thomas M. DeFrank in the New York *Daily News* informed our chapter on the South Carolina primary. As did the reporting of Jacob Weisberg in *Slate* and Jake Tapper in *Salon*. The thorough and thoughtful coverage of Lena Guerrero by Lori Rodríguez of *The Houston Chronicle* was also useful. As was Tim Russert's July 2002 CNBC interview with Karl Rove.

Subjects interviewed by the authors and John Ratliff are identified within the text. Interviews done by the authors for earlier stories and other works in progress are quoted throughout the text or used as background. Material from the authors' previously published work, and from the authors' notes and transcripts, was also used.

—LD and JR

I am indebted to my colleague on the White House beat, Alexis Simendinger, who is not only a good partner, but a diligent political observer. It was Alexis who noticed quite early in the Bush administration that Karl Rove was an influential policy, as well as political, adviser in the West Wing. She and I interviewed Rove for ninety minutes this spring, and went to his house together for the accompanying photo shoot, where she gleaned such details from him as the precise number of boxes of books the Roves brought north with them. While I'm at it, I'd like to thank my editors at *National Journal*, Charles Green and Joe Haney, as well as our publisher John Fox Sullivan and owner David Bradley, for putting out a magazine that allows reporters the time to find out what a key White House aide is doing, and the space to explain it to our readers. Our publication also puts out a daily newspaper at the two political conventions every four years. Isobel Ellis and others deserve the credit for that effort; I mention it because most of the material in this book regarding the 2000 Republican National Convention was original reporting I did while working on *Convention Daily*. *National Journal* is also fortunate enough to have the intrepid Charlie Cook and the incomparable James Barnes covering politics. During the 2000 and 2002 election cycles, I drew on the wisdom of Charlie and Jim (both from their published work in our magazine and countless times I just buttonholed them in the hallways) while writing a weekly campaign column in 2000 and in writing post–2002 election analyses. That work informed my analysis in this book of the two campaigns.

Like Lou and Jan, I also benefitted mightily from the hard work of many journalists working for other publications. It was *The New York Times* that unearthed the story of the 2001 dinner meeting between Rove and a dozen restive Republican elders. Fred Barnes of *The Weekly Standard* is the source for much of the material on the truncated tenure at the RNC of former Virginia governor Jim Gilmore. Fred also profiled Rove in an enlightening piece for his magazine that detailed the extent of Rove's involvement in national policy and well as national Republican politics.

A big tip of the hat is also due our friends half a block down 15th Street at *The Washington Post*, which has done much ground-breaking work chronicling the Bush wartime presidency. This is most true of Bob Woodward and Dan Balz, along with their regular team of White House correspondents. I tried to give credit for their work along the way, but to quickly recap: It is Woodward's book on Bush the wartime president that first revealed the delicacy of the relationship between Rove and Colin Powell. And the election night 2000 telephone exchanges between Bush and Gore first appeared in the *Post* in late January 2001, in a 40,000-word, eight-part series that was later published in expanded form in a book, *Deadlock: The Inside Story of America's Closest Election.* The primary author of that book was David Von Drehle, who is not only a peerless narrative writer, but a friend who provided encouragement for this book. In a happy coincidence, the editor of *Deadlock* was Paul Golob of PublicAffairs, who also served as one of three editors of *Boy Genius*, along with his colleagues Lisa Kaufman and David Patterson. While I'm at it, I'm also indebted to the publisher of PublicAffairs, Peter Osnos. They insisted on rather ambitious deadlines for this book, but then put in the time themselves checking, re-checking, asking for more detail, cajoling this work out of three different authors. And they did so with efficiency and good cheer. Likewise, I'd be remiss if I didn't thank my family for letting me disappear without complaint—well, the seven-year-old complained a little—over the Thanksgiving holidays to finish this project on time. Another family member, my father Lou Cannon, supplied moral support—along with fact-checking help. He is a former White House correspondent himself, as well as a writer of the very best political books.

After covering national politics for twenty years and the White House for nearly ten, the sources whose interviews I used are too numerous to cite, but I will mention a handful: On a flight from Washington to my hometown of San Francisco, Les Francis showed me the paper he'd written to try and get the Democrats to think regionally. I also interviewed the late, great Paul Tully about this in

1991, along with Democratic National Committee chairman Ron Brown and a young governor from Arkansas named Bill Clinton. I also had long conversations about it with numerous California Republicans, including Pete Wilson, Ed Rollins, and Stuart K. Spencer, an original Reaganite. Those three also helped me focus on the uneasy truce within the Republican firmament of the economic and social conservatives. The late Lee Atwater, Rollins' onetime deputy in the Reagan White House, as well as Michele Davis, another talented Reagan administration ex-pat, also assisted me in making the big mental leap from a GOP dominated by Californians to one dominated by Texans. It was a Democratic political consultant with Louisiana and Texas roots, Jim Duffy, who first predicted for me that George W. Bush would be president someday, even though he hadn't yet run for governor. Duffy had been working on a non-partisan campaign in Texas—something about a new ballpark in Arlington, Texas—and came away grudgingly impressed. Jim told me this in Memorial Stadium in Baltimore on a cold April day while we watched the quintessential Texan Nolan Ryan mow down Oriole hitters. Duffy also mentioned that Bush had a real pistol working for him, a guy with my same first name, although he spelled it with a K. It was at a racetrack in New Jersey that Mark McKinnon, the Texas Democrat-turned-George W. Bush-loyalist first talked to me about the heretofore unchronicled human side of Karl Rove. Last, and he probably won't like this because he's chary about the publication of this book, I'd like to thank Rove himself, as well as his deputy, Susan Ralston, who've dealt with me on a courteous and professional basis.

—CMC

PublicAffairs is a publishing house founded in 1997. It is a tribute to the standards, values, and flair of three persons who have served as mentors to countless reporters, writers, editors, and book people of all kinds, including me.

I.F. STONE, proprietor of *I. F. Stone's Weekly*, combined a commitment to the First Amendment with entrepreneurial zeal and reporting skill and became one of the great independent journalists in American history. At the age of eighty, Izzy published *The Trial of Socrates*, which was a national bestseller. He wrote the book after he taught himself ancient Greek.

BENJAMIN C. BRADLEE was for nearly thirty years the charismatic editorial leader of *The Washington Post*. It was Ben who gave the *Post* the range and courage to pursue such historic issues as Watergate. He supported his reporters with a tenacity that made them fearless and it is no accident that so many became authors of influential, best-selling books.

ROBERT L. BERNSTEIN, the chief executive of Random House for more than a quarter century, guided one of the nation's premier publishing houses. Bob was personally responsible for many books of political dissent and argument that challenged tyranny around the globe. He is also the founder and longtime chair of Human Rights Watch, one of the most respected human rights organizations in the world.

For fifty years, the banner of Public Affairs Press was carried by its owner Morris B. Schnapper, who published Gandhi, Nasser, Toynbee, Truman and about 1,500 other authors. In 1983, Schnapper was described by *The Washington Post* as "a redoubtable gadfly." His legacy will endure in the books to come.

Peter Osnos, *Publisher*